Why me?

**Understand why you do what you do.
Take charge of your life.**

Mary Blakely

AZURAY LEARNING, INC.
KALAMAZOO, MICHIGAN
azuray.com
e-mail: learning@azuray.com

First Edition 2000

Editor: Jan Andersen
Graphic Design: Carol A.S. Derks
Cover Design: Ed Tereshinski

Library of Congress Control Number: 00-091886
Why Not You: Understand why you do what you do.
Take charge of your life. / Mary Blakely
p.   cm.
ISBN 1882995-99-6 (Pbk)
Includes bibliographical references.
1. Success—individual & group.
2. Learning—learning styles, education, mind & body.
3. Self-actualization, self-help (psych).
I. Title

The ideas, procedures, and suggestions in this book are intended
to supplement, not replace, the advice of other trained professionals.
All matters regarding health issues require medical supervision.
The author and publisher disclaim any liability
arising from the use of this book.

Printed in the United States of America

"Ask any 10 CEOs what their biggest business challenge is, and all 11 will tell you it's communication. This book and Mary's training programs can help your company end its communication problems once and for all. Hurry up and buy a copy for everyone in your organization!"

— Charlie Wicks, CEO & President, Pro Co Sound, Inc.

"A 'must read' for all parents and educators! Truly effective educators must first know themselves, and then the children they serve. This book provides the knowledge and insight to undestand both."

— Bill McNulty, 1998 Michigan Middle School Principal of the Year

"It should be mandatory for every hospital to hand this book out to every new parent!"

— Sandra Bloomfield, Parent & Business Owner

"Great book! Mary Blakely's techniques and knowledge supplied me with the tools I needed to be a successful college student and now a classroom teacher. Her teachings transcend all learning modalities and give hope to those students who never believed they could be successful in school."

— Derek Boik, Middle School Teacher

"Mary is a most valuable referral source for my neuro-psychology practice. Her focus on developing individualized therapeutic interventions which employ each patient's receptive-expressive strengths is both unique and effective. I am pleased that she has incorporated her wealth of knowledge and many years of experience into this book."

— Ennis Berker, Ph.D., Neuropsychologist

"This book goes beyond just providing insights into how we think and behave. It gives us tools to take the next steps for healthier living and successfully managing life's challenges."

— D.J. O'Bryant, O.T., Chronic Pain Therapist

DEDICATIONS

■ ■ ■

When I think about the people who have been in my life, I am reminded of the famous movie, "It's A Wonderful Life." If just one person had been missing, I would be a different person than who I am today.

I wish to dedicate this, my first book, to the following people:

■ To my parents and sister—who gave me the family foundation and launched me into discovering life and love. Special thanks to Mom for teaching, loving, and nurturing me with an unwavering belief in my potential.

■ To John, my former husband—who shared 16 years of life and love with me and our three children when I was so blind and very young. Thank you for forcing me to open my eyes and grow up.

■ To Chad, my very wise and oldest child—who shares my work space and holds the "vision." Thank you for continually nurturing, teaching, and strengthening me and many others with your gentleness, love, compassion, humor, and wisdom. You support and enrich my soul.

■ To David, my strong, determined, loving son—who has a natural ability to reach, attract, and influence people. You possess a rare inner strength and determination to successfully meet life's challenges. You have always been, and continue to be, my inspirational teacher.

■ To Kara, my daughter, best friend, and "buddy"—who reaches my little girl and continually shares many moments of life's growing pains, adventures, loves, and joys. You are my special gift, wrapped in sparkling beauty. Your love, hugs, talents, poetry, playfulness, and grace light up my life.

■ To my close friends Jan, Suzi, Angie, Thea, and Chris—who belong to the inner tribal circle that continually supports and surrounds me with love and encouragement.

■ To Nancy, Vickie, and Jennifer—who helped carry the vision.

■ To Dick—peace, joy, love, and doves always.

■ To Greg, my dear friend—who always accepts me as I am.

■ To Snowman—for just being here.

■ To Rosie, my special teacher and friend—who continually reminds me to "keep the focus. "

■ To DJ—who is my very special partner in love, play, work, and life. You fill my life with unconditional love and effervescent, spontaneous joy! I have found my home.

■ To all of you who touched my life…and

■ To all the Hummingbirds who brighten my day!

ACKNOWLEDGMENTS

■ ■ ■

Special thanks and recognition to:

■ Jan Andersen of Beyond Words, Inc.—my dedicated editor, who lovingly cut, rearranged, and polished my printed voice.

■ Carol Derks of derkstudio—my graphic artist, who created a warm, clean, easy-on-the-eyes layout and graphics to accompany the printed words.

■ Ed Tereshinski—who created the perfect cover.

ABOUT THE COVER

■ ■ ■

BY ED TERESHINSKI

When I offered to design the cover of this book, I was actually doing it for myself—and all those with similar challenges. It's a way to say "thank you" to Mary Blakely and acknowledge what she has done for our family.

A few years ago my son, Eric, was struggling in school. My wife and I took him to be evaluated by Mary. I could see many of the same patterns in him as I saw in myself—and then some. Eric's self-image was suffering and he wasn't following the rules in his classroom. What became very clear, after spending time with Mary, was that our son was an amazingly bright, creative, Kinesthetic-Visual-Auditory learner who was having difficulty learning in a primarily auditory setting. We needed to help rebuild his self-esteem so he could enjoy school again.

However, I felt I couldn't help Eric unless I helped myself first. At 40 years old, I wanted to know why things happened, what held meaning for me, and what held me back. I needed to take charge of my life and accept my weaknesses. As I started to let go of what limited me, Mary's book strengthened my belief in the strong message: "Why Not You? You create your own destiny!"

TABLE OF CONTENTS

■ ■ ■

CHAPTER 3: THE MIND & PROCESSING PATTERNS 41-76
The six different patterns people use to process information. How processing patterns affect how we think, act, and communicate. Two particularly challenging processing patterns.

CHAPTER 4: SENSORY INTEGRATION & THE MIND 77-92
Sensory Integration: what it is, why it is important, and how it can be enhanced. How physical development affects learning. A look at ADD/ADHD.

How love and fear affect us emotionally, physically, and
mentally. How we handle power.

How beliefs affect our lives. How to identify and
change them.

Chapter 6

Chapter 7

Chapter 8

Chapter 9

PREFACE

■ ■ ■

Most of my life, I have asked the question, "Why?" "Why did he do that?" "Why did that happen to her?" "Why did I do that?"

I can recall seeing a picture of Ann Landers in the newspaper when I was eight years old and thinking, "Someday I am going to do what she does." When I was old enough, I spent hours reading about how real people overcame obstacles in their lives. Later, I went to college and studied special education and psychology. After teaching for 15 years in junior high special education and regular education classrooms, I decided to leave the public school system and create a learning center. Today, the learning center gives me the opportunity to spend my days doing what I love to do—helping people of all ages to discover their passions and realize their hopes and dreams.

I've always known that I would write a book, but I didn't know what I would write about. Now I realize that this book was being created within me all along. My life experiences and observations fill the following pages, even when I don't mention them overtly. *Been there, Done that, Got the Tee Shirt,* would have been a good title for this book! I have come to believe that our best teachers—whether they are in the teaching profession or not—are those who had to learn it first for themselves.

ABOUT THIS BOOK

This book is meant to serve as a tool for many different people. Since we each have our own faiths and beliefs, you need to read it through the lens of your own experience. It is not my intent to persuade you to perceive life from my point of view. Rather, when I present my thoughts, experiences, and explanations, I am offering different tools and techniques to help you develop a discerning eye for your own truth.

There are many times in this book when I say, in essence, "You create your own life." I do not mean that you created your physical life. Rather, I believe there is a divine spark inside each of us that supplies the wisdom, power, energy, and force we need to live. As we recognize and tap into that spark, we are able to communicate with our authentic selves and bring into reality what we truly desire.

When I use the word "victim," I am not referring to someone who is the victim of a crime or a catastrophe; that discussion would require a whole different book. Instead, I am referring to *the state of mind* when we believe we are victims—when we are focused on believing we don't deserve to have enough in life. Although our thoughts contribute to the creation of our experiences, there are many times in life when we have to let go and experience the ride. During such times we may turn to our spiritual and religious beliefs, realizing that our understanding is limited about the awesome orchestration we call life.

Throughout this book, I combine the childhood years of K-12 education with our experiences as adults. No matter how much we think we've grown up, we still are products of those formative and often difficult school years. It is very easy to fall back into the old patterns that we developed many years ago. As adults, these patterns can have a powerful negative or positive influence on our individual and global relationships, careers, families, health, educational progress, and productivity.

Finally, I suggest you use this as a workbook or a reference book. Mark it up. Scribble notes and questions in the margin. Think about, sort through, ponder, and apply the information and tools it contains. If what I say in these pages leads you to a greater understanding of your authentic self and others, then I have achieved my goal in writing this book.

INTRODUCTION
YOU ARE THE WEAVER

■　■　■

The metaphor is old—at least as old as the loom itself. You are the creator and weaver of your life's tapestry.

But maybe you didn't receive very good instruction when you were originally learning to weave. Or maybe you feel like you're "all thumbs" when you try to create something beautiful. Or maybe you just don't understand how the loom works.

This book is a guide to weaving an exciting, wonderful life. It can help you examine, unravel, and rearrange the threads of your life's tapestry. It contains tools for mending the holes where stitches were dropped and ideas for developing new patterns in your life's design.

As you create your life's tapestry, you are continuously weaving together many threads of experience into different patterns. You will never see the finished product. But you will have the joyful experience of doing the weaving, always constructing something new until you run out of thread.

As you read and work with this material, you will...

- Learn how to step back and see the whole picture behind many of life's illusions and dramas.

- Understand yourself, your partner, your children and grandchildren, your friends and coworkers, and even your enemies.

- Learn how to rekindle your passion for what you truly love to do.

- Learn how to take control of your fears.

- Identify your beliefs and how they affect your experiences.

- Discover how you learn most effectively.

- Improve your communication skills.

You are the weaver. Your life is the tapestry you are creating. I hope this book helps you with the weaving process.

.

CHAPTER 1
A FORMULA FOR SUCCESS

■ ■ ■

"The world of tomorrow
belongs to the person
who has the vision today."

∼ Robert H. Schuller ∼
EVANGELIST & AUTHOR

What makes a person successful?
Marilyn King—a former Olympic pentathlete, inspiring speaker, and good friend—shared her formula for success with me a few years ago. She identified three ingredients that are required for anyone to succeed. The formula made so much sense that I asked Marilyn for her permission to begin this book with my explanation of the formula.

PASSION
+ VISION
+ ACTION
_____

SUCCESS

Passion is what gets you up in the morning and makes you excited about your day.

Vision is your mind's ability to picture or visualize yourself experiencing the reality you choose to create.

Action is the effort that brings your passionate vision into reality.

PASSION

The first ingredient in the formula is **Passion**. Passion is what gets you up in the morning and makes you excited about your day. Time seems to fly by, and you don't even notice it. Passion involves your heart's desire. It awakens you, fills you with energy, and puts a gleam in your eye. Living your passion involves doing what you love to do, what your soul chooses.

How many of us, when we were children, had visions of achieving our passion? Some of us dreamed of becoming world-class ice skaters or NBA basketball stars. As we grew, our passions grew with us. Perhaps your passion now is to catch a big fish, climb a very tall mountain, buy a shiny red sports car, or start your own business. This passion feeds your soul. Whatever your passion is, you must be able to envision yourself living it—or you may never act on it and see it become a reality.

VISION

The second ingredient of success, **Vision**, is your mind's ability to imagine or visualize yourself experiencing the reality you choose to create. What you think about the most, you will have or become. You will draw that experience to you, regardless of whether it is positive or negative.

So when you see yourself accomplishing a certain task, or imagine something positive that you really desire, you are programming your mind and body for success.

Successful people use visualization to create their success. They know how important it is for them to focus on what they want in life. The following is Marilyn King's true story of how she used visualization to create what she wanted to experience in her life.

> **What you think about the most, you will have or become.**

■ Marilyn's Story

"I built my life around my Olympic quest. I had one particular image, one vision that sustained me. I pictured myself walking into the Olympic stadium in Munich, Germany, wearing the U.S.A. uniform I had admired since I was in junior high. On days that it was so cold and rainy outside when I woke up, and I was tempted to crawl back under the covers, I would lie back in bed, close my eyes for a moment, and envision myself at the opening ceremonies in my U.S.A. uniform. After just a moment with that image, I would be excited again. I would pop out of bed and dress warmly for my morning run, happy to be training for the Olympics. My hard work paid off. I made the Olympic team by one-tenth of a second and qualified for the third and last pentathlon spot." [1]

Just like Marilyn King, many of us have dreamed about winning some event. Every spring, Little Leaguers around the world have the dream of hitting the game-winning home run. For some, it even happens. Billy can feel the ball connecting with the bat, the beating of his heart inside his chest as he runs the bases. He can hear the roar of the crowd cheering him on. What a vision! He has passion for the game and he focuses on his vision, believing it will happen. Then, because he believes in his ability to hit a home run, he takes the action needed.

ACTION

Action is the third and final ingredient in Marilyn's formula for success. Action is the effort that brings your passionate vision into reality. Without action, passion remains only a hope, a dream, or a wish. Because Billy believes in his vision of success, he can take the necessary action. His mind and body work together to create the strength and accuracy needed to hit a home run. Yet, if he doubts his ability to hit the ball hard enough, he might not put enough strength behind his swing.

You've got to know it to show it.

You've got to believe it to see it.

THE WHOLE PICTURE

All three of the these ingredients—Passion, Vision, and Action—are needed to achieve success.

- **Passion + Vision:** Without Action you may stay in the dreamer state, telling yourself "Someday I'm going to… I really wish that I could…" Many people dream their lives away and are too afraid to act on those dreams.

- **Passion + Action:** Without Vision you can become a workaholic. You continually spin your wheels and work hard, but without a specific direction or a goal in mind. Without a goal coming from within yourself, you won't see yourself accomplishing that goal. You end up busily working your way toward something undefined. If it's undefined, you can't see it—and if you can't see it, you can't focus on it as your goal.

- **Vision + Action:** Without Passion you may burn out. You need Passion to continually feed your Vision and Action. Without Passion, your desire or conviction to achieve your goal can fade away when the going gets tough or your vision seems lost.

Athletes have known about the power of visualization for years. They focus on winning and see themselves crossing the goal line or making the foul shot.

Many professional sports teams hire trainers to help them use visualization—to program their minds and bodies for success. As a hypnotherapist, I have worked with many athletes who want to improve their performance. Too often, though, they do not experience the success they desire because they focus on their fears rather than their goal.

FEAR & SUCCESS

How do fear and negativity affect success? Here are two examples.

■ *Case Study #1: The Diver*

I recall a diver who was afraid of hitting her face on the diving board whenever she did a back dive. She wanted to overcome her fear of diving backwards by programming her mind and body to make the perfect dive. Her subconscious mind needed to erase the negative thoughts generated by her fear of hitting her face.

We changed her thoughts to a positive belief in her skills, which allowed her to see herself diving perfectly and taught her to trust her body to make the perfect formation. By programming her mind and body for success, not only did she make a perfect dive and overcome her fear, she won the event.

She wanted to make the perfect dive (Passion). She focused on her goal of diving perfectly (Vision). Then she took the necessary risk (Action) because she believed in her ability. She was successful, and the judges gave her performance a score of ten!

■ *Case Study #2: The Golfer*

Another athlete, a golfer, came to see me for help with stress. He couldn't understand why he always choked when he was playing in a tournament. He kept saying to himself, "I should be able to hit the ball better than I do. I should be better than I am in tournaments. I

don't seem to have any problem when I play alone or with my friends." The "shoulds" he kept repeating indicated that he was feeling guilty about not doing well in the tournaments.

"Shoulds" come from others' expectations and are based upon some type of guilt. I asked him why he took up golf in the first place. He told me that he'd loved golf ever since he was 10 years old. He loved the freedom of being on the golf course, the wind in his face, and the feeling of power when he hit the ball. He had found his passion. So why wasn't he performing well in tournaments?

*When he was just playing golf, his passion, his mind, and his body were working together. When he performed in tournaments, however, he buried his passion under his **fear of not being good enough**. He didn't want to disappoint his family and friends. So he focused on his fear of failure rather than on his passion for the game. He would say to himself, "Don't mess this one up. Don't hit the ball over to the right." By focusing on his fear of making a mistake, he was actually programming his subconscious mind to do exactly what he feared.*

POSITIVE FOCUS

If I tell you not to think about flying elephants, what do you see in your mind? You can't block the thought, even though I told you to. The same holds true for the word "*don't.*" "I don't want to eat that donut." What is your subconscious mind focusing on with that statement? It sees you eating the donut! Thus, your subconscious focuses on what you don't want, instead of what you really want.

The subconscious mind doesn't understand "don't." Instead of saying, "Don't shut the door," say instead, "Please keep the door open." Your subconscious will see the door remaining open instead of the door being shut. Too often, our negatively stated thoughts or our fear of failure cause us to focus on exactly what we wish to avoid. So be careful what you place your focus on. It is likely to come true!

To program your mind and body for success, **always focus exactly on what you want to have or experience**. Visualization is very literal. It can work for you or against you, so make sure that what you focus on is what you **really** want.

Marilyn King used visualization to see herself as an Olympian. As she described in her story earlier, she experienced exactly what she had focused on—being on the team and marching in the opening ceremonies.

■ *Marilyn's Story continued...*

> *"Yes, I did get to march in the opening ceremonies as I had envisioned, but my left ankle was heavily bandaged. You see, I chipped a bone while practicing long jumps in the Olympic stadium. My injury was severe enough that I was unable to compete in the Games. What I had imagined on all those cold mornings, however, had come true: I was on the team and I did march in the opening ceremonies."* [2]

Marilyn kept her passion to be in the Olympics and overcame many obstacles in her life in order to manifest her dream. She continued to train for the next Olympics, to be held in Montreal four years later.

■ *More Of Marilyn's Story...*

> *"I was more determined than ever. I trained daily and kept the vision of competing in the Olympics in the forefront of my mind. Again, my hard work paid off. I placed thirteenth in the pentathlon in Montreal in 1976. I was proud, and knew that I could do even better...*

■ *Tragedy, then victory*

> *Moscow 1979—All went according to plan until nine months before the Olympic trials... I was in a terrible automobile accident and injured a disc in my back. As a result, I lay on my couch month after month unable to get up, to shift positions or turn over. For four months I was in pain from the back of my neck down to my heels... So I started training from my bed.*

I got films of the world record holders in each of my five events. Every day in my one-bedroom apartment, I propped myself up, and when the pain subsided, I looked at those films. Day after day, over and over again, I watched them flicker on the wall... And when I had had enough, I lay back and mentally rehearsed what I had seen, going through each event, step by step in my mind. I told my muscles what they should be doing and sent them the signals they'd need later.

To make a long story short, I finally competed in the Olympic qualifying meet and took second place at the Olympic trials. I won't say that what I did was impossible, because I did it. But anyone who knows what it takes to train for a pentathlon—the sheer, overwhelming physical effort—knows that it's unlikely to be done from where I had been just months before—on my bed, unable to move." [3]

> **"Great achievements are possible for ordinary people like me because passion is our energy source and we have a clear image of our goal."**
>
> — Marilyn King,
> Olympic Athlete

Marilyn King knew what it takes to win. She believed in herself and kept her passion alive. Today, she is as passionate about her vision of world peace as she was about her vision of being an Olympian. Marilyn shares her experiences by speaking to educational and corporate audiences throughout the world with her programs, Sustained Peak Performance and Ordinary People Doing Extraordinary Things. (More information about Marilyn King can be found on page 225 in the Appendix of this book.)

BURYING YOUR PASSION: JUST SURVIVING

If we believe that these three ingredients—Passion, Vision, and Action—are needed to have success, which one is missing in so many adults and children who do not feel successful? Passion. **Living in fear and believing that we are victims supports the belief that life dumps on us. With this belief, we become survivors and put our focus on our survival, not our passion.**

When I work with adults trying to make it from one paycheck to another, I see a belief system based on the fear of not having enough. "We never can afford what we really want. Why think about it?" Or, "Man, I never seem to get ahead." These people don't trust that life will ever be different. Their lives are a constant treadmill, where their goal is just to survive and make it to tomorrow. They lose or bury their passion by focusing on their belief that they're victims—that they'll never have or be enough.

■ *Case Study #3: Living With Buried Passion*

One woman who came to our center stopped believing in the goodness of life a long time ago and buried her passion under her fear. She was very depressed and she had very little energy to direct toward her future. As a single mother who worked all day, even the thought of believing that her life could change was just too overwhelming for her to face. "Nothing ever works out, so why bother? I have all I can do to make it through each day. I don't need to go believing in rainbows." She also shared that she, "...got nothing good out of life except my two children."

When I asked her what kind of example she believed she was setting for her children, she told me that she supports them and tells them that they can do anything they want in life. She had buried her own passion, yet she still believed that her children could do and be anything they wanted to in life. Will this mother be able to teach her children to trust life and to believe in their dreams? The last I heard, she was still choosing to stay with a man who abused her.

This mother is an example of someone who sees herself as a victim in life. She believes that life will continue to deal her a bad hand. Thus, she lives every day as a victim, struggling to survive into the next hard day. She is a survivor, too busy focusing on getting by each day to include passion in her life.

Remember, what we think about the most is what we will have or become. Because this woman is stuck in a struggle to survive, she is putting all of her energy into her fear rather than her future.

JUDGMENT & PASSION

Even very young children can learn not to trust and believe in life. I once knew a seven-year-old boy who slept with a gun under his pillow, afraid of the people who constantly stopped by to purchase crack from his mother. Because this child learned that you can't trust others and you have to take care of yourself, he was too busy trying to survive to believe in his childhood dreams. When I asked him what he wanted to be when he grew up, he looked down at the floor and answered, "Alive."

We can also lose our passion when we allow ourselves to believe someone's negative opinion about us.

We can also lose our passion when we allow ourselves to believe someone's negative opinion about us. Many people stop believing in themselves at an early age, having learned from the adults who judged them that they just don't measure up to other people's expectations. Yet, we all want to feel secure, be accepted, and know that we are enough.

Suppose Joey is brought into this world by loving parents who want him. He grows up thinking that he's the center of the world. Then he overhears his Uncle George talking to his father one day. "You know, Joey just doesn't seem to be as coordinated as his brother Charlie. I just don't think he's going to be the football player you thought he'd be. He's pretty slow."

Without consciously thinking about it too much, Joey begins to believe that he may not be good enough to play sports. Over and over again he hears what others say about him being slow, until he begins to believe that he is not good enough. By the time Joey reaches age five, he is well on the way to having developed his emotional foundation for the rest of his life. His belief is, "I'm too slow to be good at anything." We can only hope that Joey's loving parents will create a positive environment where he feels loved and safe enough to risk reaching out into the world, ultimately overcoming his negative belief that he is too slow to achieve.

Today, too many children have homes where they are not given the love and support they require; they don't feel the world is a safe place. Many children are told repeatedly by their parents that they are stupid or lazy.

■ *Case Study #4: "Dumber Than A Stump"*

One man had tears streaming down his face as he shared with me how his father used to yell at him almost every day. "You're dumber than a stump. You'll never amount to anything, kid." He grew up believing what his father said to him and failed his classes. He quit school, believing that nothing mattered since he was so dumb.

It wasn't until he was in his early thirties that he finally discovered he could learn when the information was taught in a way he could understand. Fortunately, he continued to believe in himself. After completing his high school education, he pursued a career in forestry.

Imagine the difficulty of succeeding and keeping your passion if you come from a dysfunctional family where physical and emotional abuse is common. Many parents who come from childhoods with emotional or physical wounds will project their pain onto their children. Without help, some may even become abusive parents who remain stuck in the dysfunctional behavior and attitudes of their childhoods. Then the pattern continues with their own children, carrying forward the emotional and physical pain which supports the belief that they are not enough to be loved.

In addition, the divorce rate in the United States results in too many children struggling with the belief that they caused their parents' divorce because they were bad or unlovable. This is another way in which adults' problems are passed on to our children, and our children end up carrying the adults' pain.

JUDGMENT IN EDUCATION

Consider how these experiences can add to the burden of children in the classroom who have learning challenges. Their families have already led them to believe that they aren't good enough or smart enough. Then school—the very place where these children hope to succeed and feel good about themselves—can be the place where this belief is reinforced.

Frowns, smiley faces, or letter grades determine if students are good or bad, smart or dumb. Many children who struggle with learning processes buy into these labels and become victims. They may make statements like, "Why bother, I'll just flunk it anyway. Nothing ever goes right for me." Or, "That teacher just doesn't like me." These statements reflect low self-esteem and a fear of not being "enough."

Some students will decide to quit school rather than be exposed to the pain of feeling stupid or being told time after time that they aren't "living up to their potential." These children might grow up blaming their problems on their bosses, mates, and friends. Sadly, they may continue to focus on their failures, becoming blind to the many positive opportunities that life offers.

I believe that most teachers really care about their students; they work hard to help them achieve. However, there are still some teachers who use negative techniques to motivate students to perform. Negative motivational techniques damage a student's self-esteem and, in the long run, they don't work. The memory of feeling like a failure in school is always at the top of the list when I discuss past fears with a group of adults.

Think for a moment about a time when a teacher embarrassed you. Remember what was said? How did you feel? Most of us can remember such an event in vivid detail. When an adult, such as a teacher, doesn't see us as enough, it can affect us all the way into adulthood.

One man shared with me how almost every teacher said to him, "You're just not working up to your potential." He said that he felt as though the words were stamped across his forehead for the rest of his life. Those words still haunt him today.

Another man shared how painful it was when his English teacher mimicked his stuttering in front of his classmates. And I can remember how mortified I felt when my short-tempered fourth-grade teacher grabbed me by my ear and led me up to the front chalkboard to do a math problem that I had missed. I was afraid of math for a long time after that experience.

I suspect that almost every adult has at least one embarrassing or negative experience in their memories of school. Belittling students or embarrassing them in front of their classmates can cause very deep wounds that may damage their self-esteem for the rest of their lives. Every week I meet adults who still carry shame and humiliation from the labels given to them by their classmates, teachers, and parents— labels such as *dumb, retarded, Sped, slow,* and *stupid.*

> "We must learn who we are instead of telling ourselves who we should be."
>
> — John Powell, S.J.

■ *Case Study #5: The Dunce Hat*

A very successful businessman came in to see me for help with his high blood pressure. He shared with me how he was placed in the back of his fourth-grade classroom with a dunce hat on his head because his teacher said he was dumb and would never succeed.

He had spent the rest of his life trying to prove to everyone that he could succeed. His high blood pressure indicated the amount of stress and anger he felt from always trying to be enough. Even though the outside world thought of this man as a successful businessman, he didn't believe that he was. He was focused on the past, and had spent most of his adult life trying to prove his fourth-grade teacher wrong. When I asked him what his passion was, he said, "To feel successful." When I told him that he already was successful in his business and life, he replied, "Then why don't I know it?"

If you don't believe it, you won't see it. *This man couldn't see himself as being successful because he was focused on the past—that dunce hat, that thoughtless teacher, and that feeling of pain inside his chest when she called him dumb.*

SOCIETY'S JUDGMENT

Individuals are not the only ones who label and demean a person. Our society is set up to continually test, judge, and label people in order to see if they measure up to the norm. Are they above or below "normal"? Are they just average? Even at birth a baby is measured and weighed to see how he or she compares to the norm.

Too often, we place so much focus on the label that we forget there is a living, feeling person behind the label. The following true story shows how labeling and judging an individual drastically affected his life.

◼ *Case Study #6: His Name Was James*

His case folder was thick and full enough to be carried with two hands. The words, "Not Testable," were stamped on the cover in huge black letters. The file was packed with one incomplete test after another, confirming that this boy could not be tested. James was labeled schizophrenic and put on drugs at the age of eight.

Due to pressure from the boy's father to find more help for his son, a young intern was finally assigned to James' case. Nobody else at the learning institute really had the time to devote to the father's request.

The father told the intern that his son led a normal life until he had a kindergarten teacher who had just graduated from college. James liked to touch everything. He especially liked to feel the nylons on his teacher's legs when he sat next to her at story time. He also "drew inappropriate pictures of the male anatomy," according to a sexual pervert report the teacher filed on James midway through kindergarten. His teacher felt that James' behavior was not conducive to the classroom environment and would be a bad influence on the other children.

James was sent to a mental institution and labeled schizophrenic by the end of that year. His mother left his father due to the unbearable pressure of a small, judgmental community pointing its finger at each of them. If this sounds like something out of the 1920s, consider the fact that this all occurred in 1969.

By the time James met the young intern, he talked parrot talk, rocked, banged his head, and spoke to people you couldn't see.

Something inside the intern told her that there was more to this boy. She went through his entire folder searching for the answers and discovered that James had lived with several roommates while he was at the mental institution. One spoke parrot-talk, one rocked, one banged his head, and his current room- mate talked to people you couldn't see. She believed that he had learned his behavior from his roommates in the institution.

Whenever she sat down with James to work on his alphabet, he went into a high-pitched voice yelling, "No! Can't do! Can't do!" Something behind James' big brown eyes told her otherwise. Since food seemed to be the only thing she could use to get him to open up and try, James had to complete his work before he could go to lunch. Thus, James and the intern spent many weeks eating late lunches together.

Then one day, James' protective wall began to crack, and she discovered the truth. It happened when James was working with her on his alphabet. He was so agitated over not being able to go to lunch on time that he blurted out all the alphabet sounds correctly. James stopped, realizing what he had just done. Angry and afraid that she knew "the secret," he backed into a corner where he slumped over on the floor, sobbing.

The intern went over, put her hand on James' shoulder, and comforted him, telling him that it was all right. His big brown eyes full of pain looked up at her. Then he nodded his head. From that moment on, he started to open up more and show her the real James. He even laughed and sang songs with her. By the end of her internship, it was obvious that James could be tested. He could even read and understand the teacher's manual!

James had sacrificed himself in order to survive in a world that controlled, labeled, and took him away from his parents—just because someone decided that he was not a "normal" kindergartner. His parents were told that those in charge knew what was best for James, and they were convinced that he needed to be put in the institution. From then on, James' life was controlled by the "people in charge." The only way James could survive was to play their game so well that he would be left alone.

James was assigned to the learning institute's program in order to appease his father's diligent efforts to get his son more help. But the program only served children up to age 15, and James was turning 14 in the spring. So even though the young intern proved that James was intelligent, it was decided that he still didn't have the necessary social skills that would allow him to continue at the learning institute. Of course, he hadn't had appropriate role models in the institution to teach him how to act as a "normal" child.

Thus, James' folder was stamped "Testable & Antisocial," and he was returned to the mental institution. Many of the supervisors muttered their disappointment with sentences ending in words such as, "…a waste, …too bad, …unfortunate case."

On the intern's last day, James gave her a wadded up piece of paper and ran out the door. One side of the paper was totally covered with black crayon scribbling—all except for the bottom right corner. In that corner was a very tiny red heart the size of a dime.

As you may have guessed, I was the intern who had the opportunity to work with James. Although I never saw James again, I believe he was my teacher. It is because of him that I devote my life to helping people today. Our society buried James' passion. The injustices that our society did to James affected me so deeply that I promised myself I would do something in my life to help us stop focusing on labeling and testing people.

LABELING WHAT'S NORMAL

We need to see and understand people instead of the labels imposed on them. Labels can be very damaging. They put people inside a box and bury their passions. All too often, people believe in and buy the labels they are given, disconnecting themselves from who they are inside and living out the label of bad, slow, stupid, etc. It is unfortunate that we feel so much need in our society to test and label people in order for them to receive our help. In the long run, labels can be more damaging to their overall health than whatever actual challenges, illness, or disability may be involved.

I have worked with geniuses, quadriplegics, and teenagers with acne. I have worked with housewives, athletes, and elderly patients in nursing homes. They simply want to be treated like human beings.

I believe that **people are only handicapped when they believe they aren't enough**. Many of our most admired people, labeled or thought to be below "normal" when they were young, didn't let a label or someone's judgment block their success and keep them from pursuing their passion. Instead of accepting the label and becoming a victim, they took charge of their lives. Instead of saying "Why me?," they said to themselves, "This is what I want," and "Why *not* me?"

If you think about it, "normal" is itself an ambiguous label. According to The New Webster's Dictionary, normal is defined as: *conforming to a norm, standard, regular, conforming to the standard or average of a type of group, mentally or emotionally sound.*

A very wise friend once told me, "Normal is nothing more than a setting on a dryer."

On page 19 is a list containing the names of some well-known individuals who did not let judgments and labels stop them from achieving greatness in life. Look at that list now. Would you apply the label of "below normal" to any of them?

LISTENING TO OURSELVES

Why do we believe what other people say instead of listening to ourselves? Humans are a social species; we need each other to survive and thrive. So **the opinions of others are critically important to our well-being**. It is very easy to buy into their labels and negative comments about us.

Sometimes we aren't even aware of this influence. To prove to my audiences that we all buy into beliefs of not being good enough, I will often begin my classes and seminars by asking, "How many of you can sing?" I explain to them that I just want to know for a demonstration that I will be performing a little later. If I am speaking to an audience of around 100 people, about six raise their hands indicating that they can sing.

It is interesting to see how children react to the same question. If I go into a kindergarten classroom, almost the entire class will raise their hands. In an eighth-grade classroom, the students will first check to see what their friends are saying; only the five or six students who perform in church or in the school choir will raise their hands. In high school classrooms, I see the same pattern of only five or six raised hands.

So what happens when I speak to a seminar of 90 teachers? Remember, these are people who already know about self-esteem issues and encourage their students to achieve and believe in who they are. I have yet to have more than 10 teachers raise their hands. Did I ask them to raise their hands if they were opera singers? No. I only asked them to raise their hands if they could sing. What if I had asked, "How many of you can walk?" In our society, how a person walks is not judged as harshly as how a person sings.

Can you sing?

Unless there is physical damage of some kind, all of the people in the audience have vocal cords that allow them to sing. Quite simply, they have come to believe that they can't. At some point in their lives they felt judged by someone, and they chose to believe that they weren't good singers. Perhaps someone turned around in church and stared at them when they were singing, or they sang their hearts out in front of an old friend who told them that they sounded like a frog!

If we react this way to singing, just imagine how many other negative beliefs we've accumulated throughout our lives without realizing it! We've all bought into other people's judgments about us, and we carry them with us every day.

We've explored the three ingredients for success, identified passion as the most important, and seen how we can lose or bury our passion. Now let's focus on how a person can uncover or rediscover his/her passion.

The path back is through understanding the mind/body/heart connection. When we understand this, we can see how we starve or feed our passion. Let's begin with the mind, and start by discussing our "thinking" organ—the brain.

PEOPLE WHO HAVE REACHED BEYOND LABELS & JUDGMENTS

Below is a list* of well-known people who didn't let society's labels stop them.

Thomas Edison	G.F. Handel	Eleanor Roosevelt
Babe Ruth	L.V. Beethoven	Dustin Hoffman
Pete Rose	Nolan Ryan	Robin Williams
Whoopi Goldberg	Magic Johnson	Michael Jordan
Wright Brothers	John Lennon	George C. Scott
Walt Disney	Andrew Carnegie	Steve McQueen
W.A. Mozart	Napoleon Bonapart	Lewis Carroll
Isaac Newton	Jack Nicholson	Louis Pasteur
Prince Charles	Stevie Wonder	Edgar Allen Poe
Albert Einstein	Cher	Joan Rivers
Socrates	Agatha Christie	Sylvestor Stallone
James Stewart	H.D. Thoreau	Winston Churchill
Leo Tolstoy	Vincent Van Gogh	Jules Verne
Abraham Lincoln		

* Many of these names have appeared on other lists describing various disorders such as ADD, bipolar disorder, and depression.

CHAPTER 2
THE BRAIN

■ ■ ■

"The man who can put himself
in another's place,
who can understand the
workings of other minds,
need never worry
what the future brings."

～ Owen Young ～
LAWYER & FINANCIER

Our brain is an organ that weighs about three pounds. When we put our two fists together, we can see the approximate size of our own brain. Just as with the rest of our body, if we don't exercise it and use it, we lose it. The more we exercise our brain, the better it works.

OUR BRAIN'S HEMISPHERES

Although there are many ways to depict portions of the brain, a commonly accepted description divides it into two hemispheres—right and left. **The right hemisphere controls the left side of the body, and the left hemisphere controls the right side of the body.** Imagine that someone took a magic marker and drew a line from the middle of your forehead down your torso and out your legs. This line is called the midline. There are many other midlines in our body, but we will only explore this one.

Buried deep within the brain is the corpus callosum. This is the bridge that connects our left and right hemispheres. In order to share and process neural information, neurons travel between both hemispheres by crossing over from one to the other.

The left side of our brain is where we construct our thoughts and process short-term recall; the right side is responsible for long-term recall. **For optimum learning to take place, the left and right hemispheres of the brain must be properly integrated.** This allows information to be exchanged correctly between the two hemispheres.

By age nine, most of us have discovered that we prefer to use our right or left hand. This decision is not conscious. It usually involves our neurological system choosing a dominant hemisphere of the brain. Even though some children may be ambidextrous (using both hands equally well), it would actually be better and less confusing if their brain chose either the right or left hand to be dominant. We'll explore this in more detail later in this chapter.

HEMISPHERIC DOMINANCE

There has been a lot of discussion about the importance of identifying a person's learning style in order to know whether he/she primarily learns through the right or left hemisphere. I have included enough information about each of the hemispheres so you can understand how to distinguish one from the other. Each hemisphere has a distinct pattern for integrating and processing information.

We actually use both hemispheres all the time, switching back and forth between our right and left hemisphere depending on the task. However, as we grow, our neurological system usually selects one hemisphere to be dominant. The brain chooses to "listen" to that one first, giving it preference over the other.

There are a few individuals who do not display preference for one hemisphere. They are equally adept at accessing both hemispheres and seem to do better than most people when handling sophisticated con-cepts and tasks. This lack of hemi-spheric preference may be due to a natural ability to integrate and process information from a more advanced level.

> "A thought that sometimes makes me hazy: Am I or are the others crazy?"
>
> — Albert Einstein, Scientist

On the other hand, what seems to be a dual-hemi-spheric preference pattern may result from the influence of a very strong parent or parental figure in a young child's life. For example, a dominantly right-hemisphere child may imitate the left-hemispheric preference pattern of a parent. This influence may cause the child to experi-ence a lot of stress, and even lead to perfectionism if the imitation is carried to an extreme.

Here's an example of a right hemisphere-dominant son being influenced by a powerful, left hemisphere-dominant father.

■ *Case Study #7: The Lawyer Who Was A Florist*

> *Paul was a lawyer who was highly stressed from trying to please his father, who was also a lawyer. Paul wanted to become a florist, but his father considered working with flowers to be a female's career and discouraged his son from pursuing this passion. Finally, after Paul developed ulcers, he decided to take care of himself. As part of doing this, he became the florist he had dreamed about.*

HEMISPHERIC CHARACTERISTICS

Our hemispheric dominance affects our performance; it is a significant part of why we do what we do. Below is a list of the general attributes of each hemisphere. Keep in mind that these are generalities. Each of us has our own combination of left and right hemispheric patterns.

LEFT & RIGHT HEMISPHERE DOMINANCE: TYPICAL CHARACTERISTICS

LEFT HEMISPHERE (PROCESS)*	RIGHT HEMISPHERE (PICTURE)*
Structure	Spatial
Linear	Shapes/Patterns
Details/Facts	Big picture
Phonics	Singing/Music
Reading	Art
Language	Visualization
Talking	Color
Auditory	Kinesthetic
Listening	Emotions
Directions	Creativity
Parts vs. whole	Whole vs. parts
Logical	Intuitive
Time-oriented	Spontaneous
T/F & multiple choice tests	Essay tests
Few risks	Risks
Differences	Similarities
Thinks process	Thinks pictures
Concrete	Wholistic
How?	Why?

* Some individuals are transposed. That is, the process functions usually associated with the left hemisphere are handled by the right, and the picture functions associated with the right hemisphere are handled by the left. In this book, we are describing how most people function as they use their right and left hemispheres.

RIGHT HEMISPHERE-DOMINANT LEARNERS

People who learn primarily through their right hemisphere tend to struggle in today's society. In general, a dominantly right-brained person is not highly concerned with time or organization. They enjoy creative activities. Having little interest in following someone's directions, they usually prefer to make up their own. Right-hemisphere learners understand things best when they can see the whole picture before they study the parts.

Right-brained people are usually spatially oriented and learn best through color, emotion, and movement. Many of them love unstructured creativity, gravitating to activities such as art, music, dancing, writing, and acting. They tend to use visualization and may "wear their emotions on their sleeves."

Of all the right-hemisphere clients I have worked with, I have yet to see one who doesn't ask "why." "Why do I have to know algebra anyway? I'm never going to use it." Or, "Why do we have to have so many meetings? Let's just get the work done."

If these individuals can't see the application of a task to their lives, they consider the task to be unimportant. Simply telling right hemisphere-dominant children to pick up their blocks won't get the blocks picked up. However, if you give them a reason for the task that they can understand, they will probably comply with your wishes. For example, "Pick up the blocks because Grandma is coming over and she could hurt herself if she steps on them."

Right-hemisphere learners are usually very focused on how the environment affects them. They are the ones who complain, "Can we open the window? It's hot in here." They are also spontaneous people who construct their thoughts using pictures rather than processes.

For example, when I am evaluating students' hemispheric dominance, I will ask them to use some plastic colored disks to show how they would teach me that $3 \times 4 = 12$. The picture on the following page is typical of the responses I get.

3   x   4   =   12

When I ask them if they can think of another way to teach me that 3 x 4 = 12, they usually show me this:

But when I ask them if they can think of yet another way to show me that 3 x 4 = 12, only some of them will show me this example:

3 x 4 = 12

The last example shows the **process**. The other examples are **pictures** of the concept. None of them is wrong. The first three just show how a right hemisphere-dominant person tends to handle information—by using an approach based on pictures rather than process.

Since right-brained people are usually more interested in the whole picture rather than the parts, they may recall people's faces but not their names. They like to put puzzles together by constructing the frame of the puzzle first, and then fill in the rest of the pieces. Most of them shy away from logic puzzles.

TESTING RIGHT-HEMISPHERE LEARNERS

For the most part, **people who are oriented toward the right hemisphere do better on essay tests rather than true/false or multiple choice tests**. Right-hemisphere people are naturally drawn to the gray areas in life. Their worlds are not black and white. It's usually these students who love to challenge a teacher with questions that appear to be off the wall. "Yeah, but I don't see why...." And they have a much harder time on true/false tests. For an example, look at the next case study.

■ Case Study #8: The Green Tree Frog

Bill, a right hemisphere-dominant student, studied all evening about the green tree frog—its habitat, location, and food supply. He learned that most of them live in elm trees. Bill went to bed knowing the information about the green tree frog. The next day he took a true/false test covering the information he had studied. One of the questions was:

Green tree frogs live in elm trees. True or False?

*Being right-hemisphere dominant, Bill thought to himself, "Not **all** green tree frogs live in elm trees. This is a trick question." So he marked the answer as false.*

As you can see, for right-brained people, nothing is emphatically yes or no. True or false responses are not comfortable answers for a right-hemisphere learner; there is always a "yeah, but" to be considered with anything.

Two final traits that characterize right hemisphere-dominant people are their intuition and feelings. You can't hide your true feelings from most of them; they already know how you feel. Some right-brained people are so "tuned in" that they can enter a room and know right away how comfortable they are (and how comfortable everyone else is too!).

Because of their strong sensitivity to feeling, many enjoy the thrill of taking risks and feeling the wind in their faces. **The joy of spontaneity and feeling free seems to be what true right-hemisphere living is about.** Time isn't important as long as you "get around to it." Checkbooks don't have to be balanced to the penny—you just need to be "close enough." Order means lots of piles on the desk and floor.

In a right-hemisphere world, everything happens at once; it will all be managed or it's not important.

> In a right-hemisphere world, everything happens at once; it will all be managed or it's not important.

Objects are called thingies or what-cha-ma-call-its. Details just don't matter. So how can they get anything done? Where's the order and structure? Enter the left hemisphere-dominant learner!

LEFT HEMISPHERE-DOMINANT LEARNERS

Left hemisphere-dominant learners usually enjoy structure and organization. They are often verbal and enjoy tasks that involve step-by-step procedures. Most left-hemisphere people do not mind following directions.

In the left-hemisphere world, time is to be managed and logic rules. A left-hemisphere person can get so focused on details that the world will stop until those issues are resolved.

Left-brained learners have the ability to work with parts before they understand the whole picture. Generally, they enjoy logic puzzles, word games, and anything else that involves working with pieces and looking for differences. Usually, they are also good at spelling and phonics.

One misconception about left hemisphere-dominant people is that they aren't as creative as those who are right-brained. This simply isn't true. They enjoy being creative when the creative process occurs in a structured or sequential manner. They usually prefer to create something from a pattern.

For example, a right hemisphere-dominant author usually needs a left hemisphere-dominant editor who can focus on the details needed for a book or article to be well-written and grammatically correct. Song writers often count on a left-brained person to write down all of the notes within the musical chords they create.

If you present left-brained children with a box of building blocks, they will typically use the blocks to duplicate the pictures on the box instead of creating their own bridges, houses, etc. But after they are comfortable with the structure, they may deviate from this pattern and build their own creations.

In a left-hemisphere world things are either/or, with not much in between. **These students are good at understanding and using linear processes.** It was probably a left hemisphere-dominant person who first thought of the idea of a structured learning environment called "school." Otherwise, we might still be milling around with no formal organization for our experiences!

It is wonderful to have left-brained people in the world. They help us stay on task and have more structure in our lives. Yet there is one caution needed for left hemisphere-dominant learners. In their wish to have everything in order or exactly correct, they can become perfectionists. Many left-hemispheric learners become highly stressed when they expect too much of themselves.

TESTING LEFT-HEMISPHERE LEARNERS

On the whole, left hemispheric-dominant people prefer true/false and multiple choice tests over essay tests. They prefer an either/or format where answers are clearly wrong or right. **Left-brained learners don't ponder and struggle over questions, talking themselves out of the answers.**

When left-hemisphere students have the choice to be graded on an open book test or an art project that can be applied to the information from the chapter, they seem to prefer the open book test.

People who are left-hemisphere dominant are usually wonderful at assimilating and using information. They study something, learn it, and apply it. They don't spend their time questioning and wondering about all the subtle nuances that are frequently irrelevant to the task at hand. Testing formats that take advantage of this skill are excellent for these individuals.

> People who are left-hemisphere dominant are usually wonderful at assimilating and using information.

Instructors enjoy calling on left-brained students to answer questions such as, "Who can tell me what we studied in chapter 5?" They know that a left-hemispheric student will give the precise answer needed to proceed with the lesson. Business leaders count on a left-brained person to update the rest of the group about procedures and decisions that were discussed previously.

A left hemisphere-dominant person might choose a career in accounting, law, mathematics, or research.

Careers that involve structure, details, and logical problem-solving are the most appealing to them.

Left-hemispheric learners keep the world running—fortunately! They are the ones who most easily provide details, time orientation, order, and structured plans. Left-brained people take the time to read the directions first and think things over before impulsively jumping into the void.

Here's an example of the different techniques that left- or right-brained people might use to add a column of numbers.

LEFT HEMISPHERIC	RIGHT HEMISPHERIC
6	6
3	3
6	6 → 18
5	5 3
6	6 5
+ 2	+ 2 + 2
28	28

A right hemisphere-dominant person usually sees the 6's first; they are "clump learners." They look for things that are similar. Left hemisphere-dominant people are more linear. They usually add the numbers straight down.

HOW BOTH HEMISPHERES ARE USED

Fortunately, **we all use both hemispheres for learning**, even though we have approximately a 60/40 preference for one hemisphere over the other. Right-brained people can function just fine from the left hemisphere, working on detailed financial matters when they need to. And left-hemisphere learners can be spontaneous, playful artists on the weekend. But we all feel more comfortable (and under less stress) when we process information through our dominant hemisphere. We need *both* hemispheres for optimum learning and memory.

The next case study provides a glimpse into what happens when one hemisphere is damaged—in this case, by a stroke.

■ *Case Study #9: The Store Manager's Stroke*

I once worked with a woman who was a manager in the dress department of a large store. She was a left hemisphere-dominant learner. Her duties involved working with numbers and details, organizing data, ordering clothes, and writing reports.

One day, she had a stroke in the left hemisphere of her brain. After this it was difficult for her to recall what she did that morning, yet she could remember what she did as a child growing up in Germany. She couldn't recognize numbers unless she touched them or sang a song about them. She could read an entire sentence, but she couldn't recognize one of the smallest words in the same sentence when it was taken out of context.

Color, emotion, and movement were the major tools we used to help her regain her reading and math skills. She had to learn them all over again—this time from a right-hemisphere approach—until her left hemisphere healed. More emotional than before the stroke, she found herself to be more impatient, feeling like she had lost her mind. And in a way she had... only just part of it and, fortunately, only temporarily.

Almost all teachers have seen children who temporarily block information. In this situation, information from the left hemisphere travels more slowly to the right hemisphere and vice versa. When these children are afraid or anxious about tasks they are working on, tests or judged performances of any kind can create this block.

DOMINANCE PROFILES

Our eyes, ears, hands, and feet are the primary sense organs through which we take in and process most of our information.

- The left hemisphere of the brain controls movement and receives sensory information from the right side of the body.

- The right hemisphere controls movement and receives sensory information from the left side of the body.

When we are under stress, we process information and experiences through the senses that are controlled by our dominant hemisphere (i.e., the senses on the left side for right hemisphere-dominant people, and the senses on the right side for those who are left-hemisphere dominant.)

In addition to a dominant brain hemisphere, we each have a dominant eye, ear, hand, and foot. Like the brain, these are established in the neurological system when we are very young.

People show all sorts of dominance patterns. In fact, when you put together all of the potential combinations of brain, eye, ear, hand, and foot dominance, there are 32 profiles.

When we are not under much stress, our dominance profile may switch around and adapt to a given situation. However, when we are under stress, only the dominant brain hemisphere and the dominant senses function efficiently. In that case, the senses that do not feed directly into our dominant hemisphere are less effective. This explains why, **in new learning situations, we will access and express information most easily through our dominant senses**.

CROSS-LATERAL & HOMOLATERAL PROFILES

To simplify the discussion in this section, we'll explore what can be called "pure" information processing profiles. Keep in mind, however, that many people have mixed sensory dominance. For example, their left eye and foot may be dominant, along with their right ear and right hand. Whatever an individual's dominance profile is, the fundamental concepts still apply.

CROSS-LATERAL PROCESSING

Learning occurs best when the dominant hemisphere controls all of the dominant senses—eye, ear, hand, and foot. So, we are most efficient taking in and process-ing information when the dominant eye, ear, hand, and foot are on the side *opposite* the dominant hemisphere. This is called *cross-lateral* processing. (Remember: the left hemisphere of the brain controls the senses on the right side of the body, and the right hemisphere controls the senses on the left side.)

Let's look at two cross-lateral examples. For optimal visual processing, the dominant eye needs to be oppo-

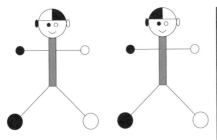

PURE CROSS-LATERAL PROFILE

Left Hemisphere
Right Eye
Right Ear
Right Hand
Right Foot

PURE HOMOLATERAL PROFILE

Right Hemisphere
Right Eye
Right Ear
Right Hand
Right Foot

PURE CROSS-LATERAL PROFILE

When the dominant hemisphere controls the dominant eye, ear, hand, and foot.

PURE HOMOLATERAL PROFILE

When the nondominant hemisphere controls the dominant eye, ear, hand, and foot.

site the dominant hemisphere. If the right brain and left eye are dominant, then visual information is easily processed because the right hemisphere controls the muscular movements of the left eye. The same is true for the relationship between the left hemisphere and the right eye.

For the most efficient auditory processing to occur, the dominant ear needs to be opposite the dominant hemisphere. Because the left hemisphere controls the muscular movements of the right ear, auditory information is easily assimilated if the left brain and right ear are dominant.

HOMOLATERAL PROCESSING

When the dominant eye, ear, hand, and foot are on the same side of the body as the dominant hemisphere, this is called *homolateral* processing. For example, if the left eye and left brain are both dominant, processing visual information is less effective; the dominant hemisphere is not controlling the muscular movements of the dominant eye.

When they are under stress, people with homolateral profiles struggle with decreased learning efficiency. In most situations, they can switch processing modes between hemispheres with no problem. However, under stress, information coming in from the dominant sense is limited because it is controlled by the hemisphere of the brain that is *not* dominant.

For instance, when both the left hemisphere and left hand are dominant, there is less sensory input coming in to the brain from the left hand. The same is true if the right hemisphere and right hand are dominant.

This is a simple, brief introduction to the theory of processing profiles—a short explanation of a much more complex topic. The chart below, by Dr. Carla Hannaford, lists the various homolateral profile combinations. If you would like to better understand cross-lateral and homolateral profiles, or learn more about the human neurological system, I suggest that you read her books, *Smart Moves* and *The Dominance Factor*. [4]

DOMINANT SENSE	DOMINANT HEMISPHERE	EFFECT ON LEARNING
Right eye	Right	Visually limited
Left eye	Left	Visually limited
Right ear	Right	Auditorally limited
Left ear	Left	Auditorally limited
Right hand	Right	Communication limited
Left hand	Left	Kinesthetically limited

© Hannaford 1997

To understand the effect of a primarily homolateral profile in real life, let's observe Julie.

■ *Case Study #10: The Blocked Writer*

Julie is a writer. Her brain is right-hemisphere domi-nant, she is right-handed, and her left eye is domi-nant. Her right ear and right foot are also dominant.

Julie loves to write stories late at night when she's cozy and bundled up with a com-forter around her.

PRIMARILY HOMOLATERAL PROFILE

Right Hemisphere
Left Eye
Right Ear
Right Hand
Right Foot

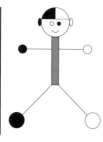

Her thoughts flow easily onto the paper as she becomes immersed in her story.

One day, Julie's English teacher decided to have her class take a timed essay test about a novel the class had been discussing. Since Julie is an excellent writer, she was thrilled to have a written test; she never did well on multiple choice tests.

But when it came time for Julie to begin her essay test, she felt like her thoughts were stuck in her head. Nothing seemed to flow. She just couldn't write down all the thoughts that she wanted to express. She kept crossing out her sentences and erasing her words. She became so nervous that she panicked. "Why can't I write my thoughts? I love to write!"

This is an example of how a homolateral profile can affect performance. Julie could write her thoughts down quickly when she was relaxed and could adjust her profile. But under stress, she became nervous.

Since her right hemisphere controls her dominant (left) eye and her left hemisphere controls her dominant (right) hand, the information from her dominant hand and dominant eye are not controlled by the same hemisphere. This means information from Julie's hand is slower to process over to her right hemisphere controlling her eye.

It needs to be emphasized that a person with a pure or partially homolateral profile will only be affected like this under stressful situations. Some techniques that seem to help homolateral learners increase their performance include these:

- Use a green transparency over visual work.
- Perform large muscle movements.
- Drink lots of water.
- Use color visualizations (i.e., imagine a certain color covering the page while reading or writing).

■ *Case Study #11: The Author's Struggle*

This section of the chapter gives me the opportunity to share a past experience that greatly affected my life. My right hemisphere is dominant, as are my right hand and right eye. So my dominant eye and hand

*are controlled by my left hemisphere, not my domi-
nant (right) hemisphere.*

*When I was in college, I had an English professor
who required many written papers. I never had a
problem with them, and I always received a grade of
at least "B." I loved to write, and I wrote my best
papers when I was relaxed and alone. However, I
really struggled when I had to write under pressure or
within a short time span. This meant I did not get as
high a grade on the papers I wrote in class as the ones
I wrote when I was relaxed.*

*One day, my professor called me into her office
and accused me of having someone else write my
papers for me, since she saw such a difference in the
quality. No matter what I said, she had her mind
made up that a person who could write "A" papers
outside of class could do just as well in class. She
lowered my grade from an A to a C. I was devastated
that someone would accuse me of cheating—especially
in something I loved to do and in which I excelled.*

JUST FOR FUN

On the next four pages are a couple of quick exercises
you can do for fun. Don't panic! Don't get stressed! No
one is grading you on these. The answers are given after
each quiz. But don't peek. It could change your results,
and then you won't learn as much.

EXERCISE: HEMISPHERIC DOMINANCE

Mark the one statement from each pair that best describes
you. There are 15 pairs in all.

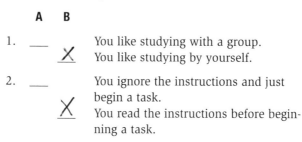

	A	B	
1.	___	X	You like studying with a group. / You like studying by yourself.
2.	___	X	You ignore the instructions and just begin a task. / You read the instructions before beginning a task.

A B

3. You often have several tasks you are working on at the same time.
___ You usually finish each task before moving on to the next.

4. ___ You will begin a task without waiting to see how other people are doing it.
You like to see how other people are doing a task before you begin.

5. You remember the main ideas better than the details when you read.
___ You remember the details better than the main ideas when you read.

6. ___ You prefer essay tests where you can explain the answer.
___ You prefer tests that are multiple choice or true/false.

7. ___ Your work space often gets cluttered.
Your work space is usually fairly organized.

8. You like team competition rather than individual competition.
___ You like individual competition rather than team competition.

9. ___ You like to choose how to perform a task.
You like to know exactly how a task is to be performed.

10. You want to see the results of your tests, but don't care about correcting errors.
___ You want to go over the test and correct any mistakes.

11. You have difficulty ignoring distractions while you are studying or working.
___ You can easily ignore distractions while you are studying or working.

A   B

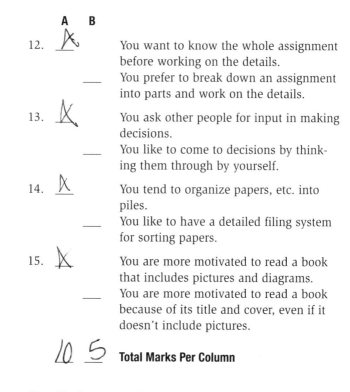

12. ___ ___   You want to know the whole assignment
before working on the details.
___   You prefer to break down an assignment
into parts and work on the details.

13. ___   You ask other people for input in making
decisions.
___   You like to come to decisions by thinking them through by yourself.

14. ___   You tend to organize papers, etc. into
piles.
___   You like to have a detailed filing system
for sorting papers.

15. ___   You are more motivated to read a book
that includes pictures and diagrams.
___   You are more motivated to read a book
because of its title and cover, even if it
doesn't include pictures.

_10_ _5_   **Total Marks Per Column**

*How To Interpret Your Hemispheric Dominance
Exercise Results*
To understand the results of the Hemisphere Dominance
Exercise, add up the total number of marks in column A.
Then do the same with column B. The column with the
highest number of marks is probably your dominant
hemisphere. Column A indicates a right hemisphere-
dominant learner; column B shows a preference for the
left hemisphere.

Don't be concerned if you have trouble identifying
your dominant hemisphere using this exercise. It is a very
simple quiz, and it may not be refined enough for some
people to determine which hemisphere they prefer to use.
If you wish, go back and review the pages in this chapter
about the left and right hemispheres. This may help you
identify your dominant hemisphere.

EXERCISE: NAME THAT DOMINANT HEMISPHERE!

See if you can identify the dominant hemisphere for each example. There are 14 statements in all. (Don't peek, but the answers are at the bottom of the page.)

1. I like to work in groups with unstructured projects. _R_

2. I like everything to be in order and in its place. _L_

3. I really struggle with true/false tests. _R_

4. I just find it easier to adjust to situations. _L_

5. I can't focus if I'm not comfortable in my seat or if it's hot in the room. _R_

6. I need to have someone show me the whole picture before I can understand how the parts fit. _R_

7. I have piles all over my desk. _R_

8. I get so frustrated trying to follow a story when it jumps from one event to another. I need to see the sequence of the events. _L_

9. I love to do logic puzzles. _L_

10. It seems like I'm always asking everyone "why?". _R_

11. I can recall his face, but not his name. _R_

12. I like to create my own way of doing things instead of copying someone's idea. _L R_

13. I really like to know the details before I put the whole picture together. _L_

14. I love my accounting job. _L_

Chapter 3
The Mind &
Processing Patterns

■ ■ ■

"I hear and I forget.
I see and I remember.
I do and I understand."

~ Chinese Proverb ~

Everyone can learn, yet each of us has our own way to learn. No one way is better than another; they are simply different. When we understand and become responsible for our learning style, our processing patterns, and how our mind operates, we can achieve greater success in all areas of life.

An orchestra needs a variety of instruments to play a composition. Different sounds occur depending on the structure of each instrument and the techniques used to play it. But the sounds are all equally beautiful. The drummer is just as important as the trumpeter. It would be absurd for us to expect a person to blow into his drum like a trumpet player. In order to play their instruments, drummers require different techniques and skills than people who play the trumpet. Yet each individual instrument is valuable to the whole orchestra. In fact, it is the harmonious blend of various instruments that creates music. Without that harmony within diversity, it's just boring noise.

So it is in life. We all must learn to play our "learning instruments" in our own special way. We must learn the techniques that can help us play the best tones or sounds in life's composition.

> **"We need to approach learning like an orchestra conductor and blend the sounds of each individual's instrument into one song."**
>
> — Mary Blakely,
>   Educator & Author

PROCESSING PATTERNS: AN OVERVIEW

Your mind is your "thinking instrument." It has its own unique way to process sensory information. You take in most of your information through three major senses: auditory (hearing), visual (seeing), and kinesthetic (touching/moving). Smell and taste, of course, are also involved. But in humans they are not considered to have as critical a role in learning and processing new information as the other three.

In addition to these three senses, the mind has three levels of awareness through which information is processed. Many different terms are used to label each of these levels. For example, people use the words "conscious," "subconscious," and "unconscious" to describe them. We'll discuss the subconscious mind later in greater detail. For now, in order to make it easier to understand the three levels of awareness, we'll refer to them as Level 1, Level 2, and Level 3.

> **You take in most of your information through three major senses:**
> - **Auditory (hearing)**
> - **Visual (seeing)**
> - **Kinesthetic (touching/moving)**

There are six possible combinations or patterns for processing information through the visual, auditory, and kinesthetic senses. Early in the development of each person's brain, his/her nervous system evolves toward one of these six as the dominant pattern for processing information. By identifying which combination a person uses, we can determine his/her structure for learning. Then we can create training and teaching programs that directly relate to that pattern.

The following diagrams show the three levels of awareness and how each level affects the kinesthetic, visual, and auditory senses.

THE THREE LEVELS OF AWARENESS

LEVEL	COMMON NAME	STRENGTH	FUNCTION
Level 1	Conscious Mind	Strongest	Level 1 is where the strongest sense is processed. Learning is easiest and fastest when using this sense.
Level 2	Subconscious Mind	Support	Processing at this level supports Level 1. The second-level sense reinforces and sorts the sensory information processed in Level 1.
Level 3	Unconscious Mind	Weakest	This is the weakest level for processing sensory information. Staying focused on a task that involves this sense is difficult.

LEVELS OF AWARENESS & PATTERNS FOR PROCESSING THE AUDITORY, VISUAL & KINESTHETIC SENSES

LEVEL 1 STRONGEST	LEVEL 2 SUPPORT	LEVEL 3 WEAKEST	LABEL
Kinesthetic	Visual	Auditory	KVA
Kinesthetic	Auditory	Visual	KAV
Auditory	Kinesthetic	Visual	AKV
Auditory	Visual	Kinesthetic	AVK
Visual	Kinesthetic	Auditory	VKA
Visual	Auditory	Kinesthetic	VAK

SAMPLE PROCESSING PATTERN—KVA

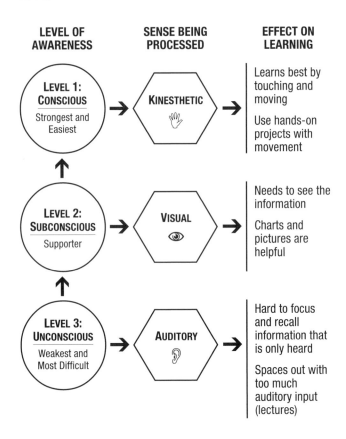

LEVEL OF AWARENESS	SENSE BEING PROCESSED	EFFECT ON LEARNING
LEVEL 1: CONSCIOUS — Strongest and Easiest	KINESTHETIC	Learns best by touching and moving. Use hands-on projects with movement
LEVEL 2: SUBCONSCIOUS — Supporter	VISUAL	Needs to see the information. Charts and pictures are helpful
LEVEL 3: UNCONSCIOUS — Weakest and Most Difficult	AUDITORY	Hard to focus and recall information that is only heard. Spaces out with too much auditory input (lectures)

PROCESSING PATTERNS & LEARNING TECHNIQUES

As you can see, we learn through a mix of our auditory, visual, and kinesthetic senses. **Teaching methods are most effective when they are directed toward the Level 1 sense of each person.**

- People who learn primarily through their **auditory** sense prefer to hear material in order to learn it. Music and tape recorders are helpful tools for them.

- **Visual** learners prefer to see what they are learning. They learn best through pictures and charts. Films, outlines, and diagrams are very beneficial to them.

- **Kinesthetic** learners prefer to learn through touch or movement in their environment. They are "doers" who learn best through experience. They need learning techniques that use physical manipulation in order to take in and recall new information.

Individuals learn most easily by processing information through their dominant (Level 1 or conscious) sense, using the Level 2 (subconscious) and Level 3 (unconscious) senses for reinforcement.

The next six pages describe the general characteristics for each of the six processing patterns. **Each person's preferred processing style utilizes all three senses to some extent.** However, the arrangement of the senses and the degree to which each is used is different for each individual.

In addition, on page 52 there is a short sensory checklist to help you determine your own processing pattern. This is a very simple evaluation, and it is only meant to give you an idea of what your pattern *might* be.

To reach everyone, we need to include all three senses—kinesthetic, visual, and auditory—when we are teaching, training, or just communicating with others.

KVA PATTERN

LEVEL 1: 🖐 **KINESTHETIC**
LEVEL 2: 👁 **VISUAL**
LEVEL 3: 👂 **AUDITORY**

GENERAL OBSERVATIONS

Traditional teaching & training methods can create significant challenges for people with this pattern.

CHARACTERISTICS

Individuals with this pattern:

- Space out with too much oral information
- Are able to focus on lectures if they can touch or move
- Do not like to give speeches
- Find it hard to tell you how they feel emotionally
- Tire easily from too many questions
- Have difficulty expressing orally what they know unless they move
- Need quiet time
- Tend to get anxious about tests and evaluations
- May get stomach aches or headaches
- Are very aware of how their body feels
- Shun scratchy or stiff clothing
- Are intuitive and usually know how you are feeling

TEACHING & TRAINING APPROACHES

To teach or train individuals with the KVA processing pattern:

- Give them a lot of hands-on experiences
- Provide time for them to touch and move
- Have them take notes or draw pictures
- Use visuals along with movement or touch
- Use book, videos, charts, and pictures
- Have them demonstrate what they know and teach it back to you or others

KAV PATTERN

LEVEL 1:	✋	**KINESTHETIC**
LEVEL 2:	👂	**AUDITORY**
LEVEL 3:	👁	**VISUAL**

GENERAL OBSERVATIONS
Traditional teaching & training methods can create significant challenges for people with this pattern.

CHARACTERISTICS
Individuals with this pattern:

- Easily remember what they have done with touch or movements
- Need frequent breaks
- Need an object to manipulate in their hands to stay focused
- Work well in groups
- May find reading and writing to be difficult
- May read best when moving
- Are good demonstrators
- Find spelling and handwriting to be difficult
- "Space out" with too much visual or detailed information
- Can be eye shy
- Can listen without focusing on the speaker
- Are not visually organized in their room or work space
- Would rather tell you than show you how they feel
- May get stomach aches and headaches
- May choose to avoid visual work
- Are intuitive and usually know how you are feeling
- Shun scratchy or stiff clothing

TEACHING & TRAINING APPROACHES
To teach or train individuals with the KAV processing pattern:

- Create hands-on experiences for them
- Act out things or create models
- Sit them near a window
- Use large and small muscle movements
- Use oral correction more than visual
- Touch them on the shoulder or back to keep them focused

AKV Pattern

LEVEL 1:	🖐	AUDITORY
LEVEL 2:	🖐	KINESTHETIC
LEVEL 3:	👁	VISUAL

GENERAL OBSERVATIONS
People with this pattern usually make good teachers and trainers.

CHARACTERISTICS
Individuals with this pattern:
- Easily memorize what they hear and move to
- Learn by hearing and discussing
- Tend to mumble and need to hear what they are thinking while they work
- Work well with background music
- Often have sloppy writing and organize their things in piles
- Easily "space out" with too much visual work
- Recall emotionally what is written to them
- Need visually spacious places to focus their eyes
- Do not like to look people in the eye
- May not keep a visually neat room or work space
- Love to share creative ideas and stories, act, and tell jokes
- Have a lot of physical energy
- Will tell you how they feel rather than show you
- May get very nervous before tests

TEACHING & TRAINING APPROACHES
To teach or train individuals with the AKV processing pattern:
- Encourage them to read written directions out loud
- Encourage them to say what they are thinking in their own words
- Encourage them to share new ideas
- Place them by a window
- Encourage written explanations
- Offer many hands-on projects
- Use oral correction more than written

AVK Pattern

LEVEL 1:	👂	**AUDITORY**
LEVEL 2:	👁	**VISUAL**
LEVEL 3:	✋	**KINESTHETIC**

GENERAL OBSERVATIONS

People with this pattern usually make good teachers and trainers.

CHARACTERISTICS

Individuals with this pattern:

- Learn by listening and discussing
- Need to orally outline what you are discussing
- Need to put thoughts into their own words
- Need to hear what they are thinking
- Usually love to read
- Tend to read out loud
- Can be easily discouraged with physical activities
- Enjoy sharing and discussing their feelings

TEACHING & TRAINING APPROACHES

To teach or train individuals with the AVK processing pattern:

- Encourage them to be problem solvers
- Use a lot of patience when teaching physical skills
- Explain physical activities in small steps
- Use charts, pictures, and figurative language
- Encourage them to share ideas orally
- Use visualization and imagination
- Avoid too many challenging hands-on projects

VKA PATTERN

LEVEL 1:	👁	**VISUAL**
LEVEL 2:	✋	**KINESTHETIC**
LEVEL 3:	👂	**AUDITORY**

GENERAL OBSERVATIONS
People with this pattern experience greater success with eye-hand tasks.

CHARACTERISTICS
Individuals with this pattern:

- "Space out" with too much auditory information
- Need to use visual aids and movements to stay focused
- Learn best from a "show and tell" approach
- Do not like to give speeches
- Need moments of silence
- Need hands-on training and teaching methods

TEACHING & TRAINING APPROACHES
To teach or train individuals with the VKA processing pattern:

- Use visual aids and movement to keep them focused
- Provide written and oral instructions
- Give them outlines to follow for lectures
- Encourage them to take notes and make maps or charts
- Break up lectures with time to move
- Use visualization
- Encourage them to move while they speak
- Allow for quiet time
- Break down physical tasks into small demonstrations

VAK Pattern

LEVEL 1:	👁	VISUAL
LEVEL 2:		AUDITORY
LEVEL 3:	🖐	KINESTHETIC

GENERAL OBSERVATIONS

Learning is easier for people with this pattern; it is the most compatible with traditional training and teaching techniques.

CHARACTERISTICS

Individuals with this pattern:

- Learn by listening and discussing
- Need to orally outline what is being discussed
- Need to put thoughts into their own words
- Need to hear what they are thinking
- Make good teachers and trainers
- Usually love to read
- Tend to read out loud
- Can be easily frustrated with physical activities
- Enjoy sharing and discussing their feelings

TEACHING & TRAINING APPROACHES

To teach or train individuals with the VAK processing pattern:

- Encourage them to be problem solvers
- Use a lot of patience for physical skills
- Explain physical activities in small steps
- Use pictures, charts, and figurative language
- Encourage them to share ideas orally
- Use imagination
- Avoid offering too many challenging hands-on projects

EXERCISE: SENSORY CHECKLIST

Now it's your turn to see if you can identify your own sensory processing pattern. Mark all of the following statements that you feel strongly describe yourself. You may have several items checked in a section, only a couple, or none at all.

KINESTHETIC

○ You learn best when you can perform a task.

○ You have trouble paying attention if you sit still for a long time.

○ You often slouch in your chair or fidget if you sit still too long.

○ You feel like you always have to be moving some part of your body.

○ Movies or books must be full of action to keep your attention.

AUDITORY

○ You talk out loud to yourself to solve problems or vent anger.

○ You need to hear yourself say things in order to remember them.

○ To memorize information, you need to repeat it aloud or to yourself.

○ You would rather listen to a description of something than read about it.

○ You can easily remember information put to a beat or music.

VISUAL

○ You learn best if you can see the information you need to learn.

○ You like to see charts and pictures, in addition to text, when studying from a book.

○ You are drawn to bright, colorful objects.

○ You often visualize situations in your head as you think about them.

○ You remember something better if you see it in writing.

How To Identify Your Pattern

To identify your processing pattern using this checklist, count the number of boxes you checked in each of the three sections: Kinesthetic, Auditory, and Visual.

The section with the most checkmarks is probably your Level 1 sense. The section with the second highest number of checks is likely to be your Level 2 sense. Finally, the section with the least number of marks is probably your Level 3 sense.

> "There isn't any idea I've had that I haven't put down on paper."
>
> — Isaac Asimov,
> Author & Scientist

For example, if you checked four boxes under Kinesthetic, five boxes under Auditory, and two under Visual, you probably have an Auditory-Kinesthetic-Visual (AKV) processing pattern.

Your Processing Thumbprint

The individual sensory processing pattern we each use becomes our unique thumbprint for learning and communicating. By understanding the six different patterns and how they affect the way we assimilate and express our thoughts, we can experience greater success in all areas of our lives.

When you look at the characteristics listed for each pattern (pages 46 to 51), you can see that they have their own strengths and challenges. For instance, it would appear that people with the VAK or AVK (Level 3 kinesthetic) processing pattern "have it made" when it comes to learning because these patterns are the most compatible with traditional training and teaching techniques. However, they have a big challenge with anything kinesthetic.

Visual-Auditory-Kinesthetic and Auditory-Visual-Kinesthetic individuals usually don't consider physical education to be one of their favorite classes. They would rather visualize exercising to stay in shape. Level 3 kinesthetic processors can sit for hours reading, writing, or talking on the phone. Any activity that requires a prolonged amount of time devoted to physical exercise can be exhausting. They may enjoy climbing a mountain for the beautiful view, but not for the physical challenge of it. Or they may take a leisurely bike ride to stretch their muscles; they're not really interested in seeing how many more miles they can go beyond their last ride.

Since VAKs and AVKs aren't kinesthetically oriented, they tend to experience life more through their visual or auditory senses. As a Level 3 kinesthetic processor myself, I understand how these individuals struggle with large and small muscle activities. Just threading a needle can drive them crazy! Because it was difficult for me, I chose not to take advanced typing classes in high school. I couldn't foresee any time in my life when I would need to have typing skills. Of course, if I had known that computers, word processing, and writing a book were in my future, I would have handled things differently—literally!

COMMUNICATION & PROCESSING PATTERNS

Most of us express our thoughts through our strongest sense, so it is usually fairly easy to identify each person's strongest processing sense. How? Just listen to what they say. For example:

- Visual processors may say something like, "I see what you're saying."
- Auditory processors may say, "I hear what you're saying."
- Kinesthetic processors may say, "I feel that I know what you're saying."

On the other hand, we also reveal our weakest processing sense through actions that disconnect us from others when we're trying to communicate.

- Visually unconscious processors may choose to avoid eye contact.
- Auditorily unconscious processors may have very little verbal response to your questions.
- Kinesthetically unconscious processors may squirm and fidget during a conversation.

Many bosses and employees, teachers and students, and parents and children misread each other due to the different ways in which they communicate. With this knowledge, you may begin to have a different perception about their actions. For example, you may be less likely to conclude that someone is unsociable just because he/she doesn't carry on a conversation with you when you first meet.

As you consider how processing patterns relate to communication skills, you also need to be aware that the unconscious mind (Level 3) is where our creativity and intuition abide. This is the deepest level, where symbolic language is processed with the least awareness.

We receive messages kinesthetically, visually, and auditorily. But it takes longer for messages mediated through the Level 3 sense to process through to present awareness. When we receive input through this sense, we actually "know" what we have perceived before it rises to the level of conscious awareness. This accounts for some of the intuitive experiences we all have. For example, as a kinesthetically unconscious processor, I often experience hives long before an actual event that I'm anxious about takes place.

Because it takes longer to process messages through the unconscious mind to present awareness, we are usually less effective—and often uncomfortable—with input coming through our Level 3 sense. By knowing the areas of discomfort related to each of the unconscious processing modes, you can increase your communication with anyone in your life. Here are a few guidelines to help you put your best foot forward.

KINESTHETICALLY UNCONSCIOUS PROCESSORS: VAK & AVK
These people:

- Feel things deeply, but take a long time to know what they're feeling.
- Become overwhelmed with too much physical activity.
- Prefer to have unguarded touch kept to publicly acceptable actions—handshakes, pats on the shoulder, etc.
- Consider physical connections as either bad or good, and remember them for a long time.
- May become highly frustrated with unfamiliar large- and small-muscle tasks.
- Will often tolerate or endure tension for a long time in their body.

- Can verbally talk about their feelings without consciously connecting to them through their body.

VISUALLY UNCONSCIOUS PROCESSORS: AKV & KAV
These people:
- Are often uncomfortable with direct eye contact.
- Display their emotions in their body language more than their faces.
- Are uncomfortable with on-the-spot writing exercises.
- Are able to listen to you while looking away.
- Remember, and are strongly influenced by, intense disapproving looks.
- Have trouble with cause and effect, and difficulty with inner vision.
- Relate strongly in their body by feeling what they see.
- React poorly to written corrections on anything that they have written or drawn.

AUDITORILY UNCONSCIOUS PROCESSORS: KVA & VKA
These people:
- Can be very uncomfortable with yes/no questions.
- Are uncomfortable when they're expected to answer questions related to desires or emotions.
- Need time to speak and respond.
- Require a lot of silence.
- Respond best to soft, nonjudgmental tones.
- Respond best to suggestions rather than statements or demands.
- Will often shut out others who yell at them.
- Remember for a long time what is said to them in a negative manner.
- Respond well to music.
- Need time to rest and close their eyes to rejuvenate.

TWO CHALLENGING PROCESSING PATTERNS

Of all the processing "thumbprints" people have, two patterns seem to be the most difficult to live with in today's world: the Kinesthetic-Visual-Auditory (KVA) and the Kinesthetic-Auditory-Visual (KAV) patterns.

In our society, most learning environments and institutions focus primarily on the left-hemispheric, visual or auditory processing patterns: VAK, VKA, AVK, and AKV. Each of these patterns has a strong visual or auditory sense in Level 1.

In our society, most learning environments and institutions focus primarily on the left-hemispheric, visual or auditory processing patterns.

This does not include KVA and KAV individuals, who are primarily kinesthetic in Level 1. They need to touch and move around in their environment in order to learn most effectively. These two patterns, KVA and KAV, have the most trouble achieving success in typical educational and training settings. As a result, people with these patterns often struggle more than others with learning, training, and self-esteem issues.

KINESTHETIC PROCESSORS: AN OVERVIEW

Kinesthetic-Visual-Auditory and Kinesthetic-Auditory-Visual processors are often athletes, dancers, builders, plumbers, designers, or car mechanics. They are literally hands-on people. **They like to touch and move objects.** KVAs and KAVs tend to be sensitive to their environment, and they are affected by lighting, color, and energy more than most people. Level 1 kinesthetics may also be strongly intuitive.

People who are primarily kinesthetic are large- and small-muscle movers who like to feel the freedom of movement. They love to ride fast and feel the wind in their face. They enjoy hugs and usually want to be touched or have a lot of body contact. Football players, wrestlers, hockey players, motorcyclists, and bikers are usually kinesthetically oriented individuals. Since they process most of their sensory information through their skin and sense of touch, they need to move or touch something in order to stay stimulated and focused.

Level 1 kinesthetic processors usually don't like to be bound by anything. They often choose to wear baggy, loose clothing, and they will kick off their bed covers. For some kinesthetically conscious people, the way their clothes feel is so important that they will spend hours searching for the material that feels the best on their skin—or the shoes with exactly the right fit—or the pants that are not too tight, too stiff, or too scratchy. Even tiny wrinkles in their socks or tags on their shirt collars can wreck the day for kinesthetic individuals!

For kinesthetic-dominant learners, stretching and moving their muscles after 20 minutes of sitting and listening increases their ability to stay attentive and focused.

For kinesthetic-dominant learners, stretching and moving their muscles after 20 minutes of sitting and listening increases their ability to stay attentive and focused. Those who sit or work on a task too long will space out or daydream. Although it may be difficult to create the time and space for movement, people who are kinesthetic processors may be left behind if muscle movement and/or touch are not incorporated into the learning experience.

When I ask Level 1 kinesthetics where they go when they daydream, they all seem to have a special place where they are busy *doing* something. Since our bodies actually don't understand the difference between external reality and fantasy, they believe what our minds say is going on. **When kinesthetic processors daydream, they can sit perfectly still for a longer period of time; their bodies believe that they are doing something.**

For example, David mentally worked on a science experiment in his laboratory during his company's Monday morning briefings. Kara rode her horse and practiced jumps during church sermons. And Chad practiced slap shots on the ice during college lectures. They, like many other kinesthetics, use escape or survival tactics like daydreaming to remain still in their seats.

Companies that assemble products requiring meticulous eye-hand coordination should allow their employees to exercise their bodies every 20 minutes or so. This will pay off in the long run because there will be fewer mistakes on the line, fewer health problems, and an overall increase in productivity and employee morale.

In addition, individuals who are kinesthetically dominant require more water to replenish their electrolytes. Electrolytes are the ions needed by cells to regulate the electrical charge and flow of water molecules in the body. Since kinesthetics use more energy when they move, they need to replenish the water used in this process more often.

What, essentially, does all this mean? To meet the needs of kinesthetic learners, our business and educational institutions need to provide working and learning environments with techniques and programs that include the sense of movement and touch. Teachers and trainers must include large- and small-muscle movements in all of their programs to effectively reach these people.

KINESTHETIC PROCESSORS AT WORK

For KVAs and KAVs to experience success, they need the time and space to move. Movement anchors their thoughts and stimulates their minds. They require both large- and small-muscle movements to stay focused on what they see and hear. The following case studies illustrate how these individuals can be affected in the workplace.

■ *Case Study #12: Geno, The KVA*

Geno, a Kinesthetic-Visual-Auditory processor, had been promoted and was trying to learn how to operate a new machine. His foreman touched each part and showed Geno how to use it. He summarized what he'd said, and then asked Geno if he understood what to do. Geno nodded his head, pretty certain that he'd learned what he needed to know.

The next morning, when Geno went to work, he became confused when he looked at the machine. He realized he couldn't remember everything he needed to know; he'd have to ask his foreman to explain it again. Although he had an excellent work record, Geno was afraid he'd look stupid and might even lose his job.

What neither of the people in this example realized was that Geno, not his foreman, needed to touch each part of the machine while he looked at it and heard about its function. This would have imprinted the information he was learning through his strongest sense for recall, the kinesthetic. Then, Geno needed to repeat the information back to his foreman while he touched and looked at the part again. By doing this, he would have used his visual and auditory senses to support and lock the information into his mind for greater long-term recall. By just telling Geno how to operate the machine, the foreman was trying to convey information through Geno's weakest sense, the auditory.

■ *Case Study #13: Joan, The KAV*

Joan was a Kinesthetic-Auditory-Visual processor whose boss, Kurt, sent her spur-of-the-moment memos involving complicated procedures with a lot of detail. He expected her to explain these procedures to the other employees.

Joan always had a hard time understanding Kurt's memos. She just couldn't keep her mind focused on all the details. It made her very nervous to see a page full of tiny print, especially when she needed to add up a lot of numbers in her head in front of the other employees.

Joan felt overwhelmed in her position as a facilitator. She was a hard worker and enjoyed talking with the other employees. But often, Joan didn't correctly convey the information to the other employees, and they ended up covering for her. After several mediocre performance reviews, she was laid off during a company downsizing.

Joan feels insecure with visual material since it takes her so long to understand and recall the information. To reduce stress and confusion, she needs to receive these memos early so she has time to review the material, ask Kurt questions, and grasp the big picture. Because her weakest sense is visual processing, she can't picture the details in her head unless she writes them down herself—thereby bringing them through her strongest sense, the kinesthetic.

In this case, neither Kurt nor Joan realized that her job responsibilities and the way he gave information to her did not coincide with her primary processing pattern. Joan could have been highly successful with some modest changes to her current position or in another job that took advantage of the strengths of her KAV processing pattern.

As you can see, when a company does not develop effective training and communication methods for different learning styles, it has negative results for both the employee and the company. The employee feels inadequate, frustrated, or angry. The company wastes training time and money, and it may lose someone who would have been a good employee.

KINESTHETIC PROCESSORS & MARKETING

Marketing is another area that can be positively influenced by understanding how people process information. By knowing the customer's pattern, a sales person can appeal to his/her strongest sense for processing information.

For example, when a sales person is trying to sell a car to a woman who is right hemispheric and Kinesthetic-Visual-Auditory, he should get her to sit in the car as quickly as possible. The KVA customer doesn't want to look at a glossy brochure or hear all the details about the car. She wants to feel what it's like to sit inside and imagine herself racing down the road. *After* she has touched the car and feels comfortable with it, she will be more inclined to read a brochure and possibly hear about the car's features.

On the other hand, an individual who is a Kinesthetic-Auditory-Visual processor wants to listen to all the details while she sits behind the wheel. She might even scan the brochure and check out the charts and pictures if the sales person points them out while she's in the car.

Kinesthetic customers will buy products more readily when you let them experience the product through their sense of touch.

Remember, kinesthetic processors are often strongly intuitive. They may quickly select or reject a product for reasons that are not apparent on the surface. You want to help them feel good about the product and their purchasing experience.

Many sales people lose KVA and KAV customers by talking rapidly or giving them too much to look at while making their sales pitch. Unfortunately, if they don't include the kinesthetic sense, they are likely to lose the sale. Since most good sales people like to talk, this can be difficult. If you are trying to sell something to kinesthetic customers, give them time to feel and experience the product. Then tell them about its wonderful qualities.

KINESTHETIC PROCESSORS & EDUCATION

Education is another area where understanding a person's processing pattern is crucial for individuals to experience success.

Teachers and trainers must remember that movement anchors kinesthetics' thoughts for long-term recall. When I do training lectures or educational seminars, I can tell immediately when the kinesthetic processors need to take a break and move: they start dozing off, squirming in their seats, or shaking their legs.

There is an excellent demonstration to show KVA people how necessary it is for them to move their body in order to imprint and process auditory information. I give oral directions to KVA volunteers from the audience. Then I have them repeat those directions back to me. I have yet to have any of the volunteers be able to repeat all the instructions correctly. Next, I have them perform the directions as I say them. Once again, they are asked to repeat the directions back to me in the correct order. Not once has any KVA volunteer failed to repeat all the directions back perfectly. Why?

When KVAs only hear the directions, they can't recall the information because auditory is their weakest (Level 3) processing sense. However, **if they hear the directions and perform them, they recall the directions perfectly.** They have processed the information through their strongest sense—their kinesthetic/bodies.

Here is a list of some of the most important points related to people who are primarily kinesthetic processors.

- Both KVAs and KAVs learn best by moving and manipulating objects.

- Students with these patterns enjoy learning when they are actively involved in the educational experience. The more they use their bodies, the more they love to learn.

- If kinesthetic-dominant individuals are uncomfortable in the learning environment, they'll have difficulty staying focused on their work.

- Kinesthetics need to use their large muscles when they learn new information. If they don't, they may miss a fundamental concept or process that will be built upon in future lessons.

- Level 1 kinesthetic processors need to have their on-task time broken down into 20-minute intervals. For young children, these intervals might be as short as 15 minutes.

- Seat KVA and KAV students on the aisle where they can be easily touched or tapped on their shoulders. Since these individuals tend to space out if they aren't given time to move physically, touching them gently will bring them back to the work in the classroom.

KINESTHETIC PROCESSORS AT HOME

If you are the parent, partner, boss, or friend of a kinesthetic-dominant processor, life is not dull! You will indirectly experience life through the body because that's how they experience it. Sometimes you may feel that they're going too fast and will never settle down. At other times you'll see them work themselves to exhaustion and then "zone out."

In general, kinesthetics don't enjoy just sitting and reading, talking, or watching TV all evening (unless they can channel surf). If you live or work with Level 3 auditory kinesthetics, you've probably already figured out how much oral information you can give them before their eyes glaze over. And if you live or work with Level 3 visual kinesthetics, you may wonder how it's possible for them to miss what is right in front of them.

THE MISUNDERSTOOD KVA

I believe the Kinesthetic-Visual-Auditory processing pattern is the most misunderstood of the six patterns. Very good at working with their hands and bodies, these people often have difficulty expressing their feelings. Many KVAs do not like to talk about their emotions, and they are uncomfortable with small talk. Therefore, many people consider them to be unsociable snobs with an attitude!

Many KVAs do not like to talk about their emotions, and they are uncomfortable with small talk.

Some people who are Level 3 auditory processors are so uncomfortable at social events that they need to be given starting sentences to help them talk with others. Also, most of them do not like to give speeches. Their words don't seem to flow, and they become very nervous trying to express their thoughts.

It takes a lot of energy and concentration for a KVA to bring auditory information from the unconscious (Level 3) to the conscious (Level 1) level of awareness. Thus, processing and recalling auditory information is difficult unless they use their kinesthetic sense.

If KVAs move their large muscles, words usually come out more easily. When they talk on the phone, it helps KVAs to play with the phone chord, walk around, or doodle on something.

THE KVA & EDUCATION

Kinesthetic-Visual-Auditory learners need visual information along with movement in order to understand and process oral information. Outlines, graphs, charts, and pictures may help them. KVAs usually need to take notes or draw pictures to stay focused on lectures and recall what they hear. They may become very stressed during oral presentations in front of others.

Too often, KVAs are disciplined orally, e.g., when a teacher yells at them. Since they remember forever anything said to them in a negative manner, it is better to write down corrections or behavioral rules and then go over these items with them orally. In addition, to truly learn and integrate lessons, KVAs need to be gently touched as they are corrected.

KVAs need to *see* what they're doing wrong. They will tend to develop low self-esteem if they are always corrected orally. In fact, many KVAs become selective listeners to protect themselves from negative and confusing auditory input.

KVAs learn best by demonstrating the material back to someone. When they move their large muscles by writing a word or a math problem on the board, they imprint the information. These learners need to have the opportunity to say, "Can I show you what I think you said?" when they ask for help.

By allowing KVAs to draw, hold an object in their hands while they listen to a lecture, or chew gum, they can stay focused longer on what they need to hear.

■ *Case Study #14: The Mechanic*

John was a talented car mechanic with the KVA processing pattern. He was successful with his hands-on work, but he had trouble staying focused during lectures. He found himself constantly daydreaming in class and not recalling what the teacher said. He would absent-mindedly work with his hands while he listened—taking notes or doodling on his paper.

Fortunately for John, his teacher didn't interpret this activity as boredom or inattention. She recognized that he was primarily kinesthetic and that he learned more when he was allowed to make sketches on his papers and "fidget."

THE KVA AT HOME

Many couples or families understand their partners or children better when they learn about the Kinesthetic-Visual-Auditory pattern. Because KVAs do not like to talk about how they feel, they may not say, "I love you," very often. They would rather make something, write it down, draw a picture, or share a hug.

Level 1 auditory people (AKVs or AVKs) are comfortable saying how they feel, so they may expect to *hear* "I love you" from their child or partner. However, if that person is a Level 3 auditory processor, this can lead to significant emotional pain and/or misunderstanding. "He never tells me he loves me," is what a primarily auditory person might say. Common KVA responses to this would be, "What do you mean? I'm always giving you hugs," or, "I wouldn't be here if I didn't love you."

■ *Case Study #15: The Newlyweds*

> *Barb and her new husband Don were upset with each other. Don couldn't understand why Barb was always yelling at him or giving him the cold shoulder. He knew he was attentive and faithful to her. He just couldn't understand why she was always so mad at him.*
>
> *Barb was very frustrated with Don. She didn't believe that he really loved her. She said, "He hardly ever tells me that he loves me anymore or that I look nice." Barb was mad because she wanted more attention. She wanted to hear that she was loved.*
>
> *Don was very confused. He didn't understand why Barb would doubt his love for her. "I'm here aren't I? Don't I pat you on the bottom every day when we leave for work?" As far as telling her she looked nice, Don's response was, "I wouldn't be with you if I didn't think you looked nice."*
>
> *Barb and Don learned a lot about each other when they understood how their processing patterns were influencing each others' actions and expectations. Barb, an AVK, needed to hear that she was loved. Don a KVA, thought he was showing her his love by touching her, doing things with her, and just being with her.*

People who are Level 3 auditory processors can feel a lot of emotion. (In fact, they are often too caught up in the emotion to express their thoughts.) It's just that they tend to express emotion through their bodies instead of orally. KVAs find it easier to express their emotions when they are working on a task that uses their large or small muscles, such as washing the dishes. They will also be more expressive when they are receiving back rubs or being held.

Often, Level 3 auditory people who are primarily kinesthetic **will talk about how their body feels, rather than expressing how they feel emotionally**. They may say things like, "My body feels heavy," or, "My body feels weird." A Level 3 kinesthetic person might think in response, "Well get over it. It doesn't matter. Just suck it up and go on." They don't understand that it is very hard for kinesthetics to concentrate on anything if their bodies aren't comfortable.

Parents and partners need to know something about the auditory limits of the KVAs they love. Because the auditory sense is the most difficult for KVAs to process, these individuals can become very stressed if they're asked too many questions or have to listen to long explanations. Their limit is usually three questions and no more than 20 minutes of listening before they feel auditorally bombarded. Yet, if they're deeply interested in the subject matter, they can remain focused longer.

KVAs can recall what you say to them if you touch them while you speak. But unless you write down what you want them to do before you leave, or have them demonstrate the task back to you, they probably won't remember what you said before you're halfway out the door!

> **KVAs can recall what you say to them if you touch them while you speak.**

There is one final important fact to know about Kinesthetic-Visual-Auditory people. Because our society depends so heavily on spoken communication, Level 3 auditory processors spend a great deal of time handling information through their weakest level of awareness. After doing this all day, KVAs (and VKAs) need to have time out when they don't have to listen or talk to another person. They need time away from questions and lectures to relax and integrate what they've heard. Most of them will be open to being around people again after they've had a chance to be alone and unwind.

THE KAV PROCESSOR

Kinesthetic-Auditory-Visual people enjoy and need the same stimulation of movement and touch as the KVAs, but it is often difficult for them to recall or stay focused on what they *see*. They need to move their bodies and express their thoughts out loud in order to effectively process information. (For example, think about what cheerleaders or military drill instructors do.) KAVs can be very creative; many of our most famous athletes and actors have this pattern.

KAVs have a hard time picturing and organizing their thoughts unless they can write them down or use their kinesthetic sense in some other way. People with their visual sense at Level 3 may not be good at giving directions off the top of their head. However, they will be successful if they draw a map or list the route in steps.

Because KAVs can have a hard time picturing and organizing information in conventional ways, their work space may appear to be chaotic and untidy. However, many KAV processors have a sophisticated way of organizing their things into piles. To others' astonishment, they can plunge into the "mess" and find the precise item when its needed. This is why it is very frustrating for KAVs when someone else cleans up their work area or moves their piles. Many KAVs use physical, spatial orientation for tracking and organizing. Without physically experiencing where something was put, they can lose their spatial point of reference for recalling an object's location.

There is one other potential problem for people with the KAV processing pattern. Because it is difficult for them to picture possible scenarios, these individuals struggle with cause and effect. They are not stupid or mean or uncaring—they truly may not see the potential consequences of a particular action. Many KAVs will admit that they get into trouble because it's so hard for them to visualize outcomes.

For example, teens with the KAV pattern who find themselves in trouble will say, "I don't know why I did it. I just felt it would be fun." When asked why they thought they could get away with something, many will respond, "I don't know. I guess I didn't think about it."

The next case study describes what can happen when this impulsiveness takes over.

■ Case Study #16: The Saw & The Table Leg

Mark, a KAV, is a very successful builder. Once, when he was a boy, his father placed a new electric saw on the kitchen table. Mark decided to check it out. He wanted to know how it would feel to work with the saw. In the process of "checking it out," he sawed off one of the kitchen table legs.

His parents couldn't understand why he always did outlandish things like sawing off table legs. When they asked him why he did it, his response was, "I don't know." Thinking back as an adult, Mark recalled how much he wanted to just experience what it would feel like to work with the saw. He hadn't really planned on sawing the leg off, and he still marvels at the fact that he actually did it.

Mark had to work for a very long time in the corn field to pay for his mistake. And although he has other similar tales to share about his childhood, he never sawed off another table leg!

People with the KAV processing pattern seem to understand cause and effect best when they either act out a scene or draw a picture about it. Many KAVs need to experience a process in some kinesthetic way before they can picture the outcome in their mind. It helps if they can also hear someone describe the possible results, or if they talk about the situation with a nonjudgmental person.

For children to learn about cause and effect, they need to *experience* the potential results of an action first-hand. The next case study shows how one family handled a potentially dangerous situation.

■ Case Study #17: Justin & The Busy Street

When Justin was six years old, his parents couldn't get him to stop riding his bike in the busy street in front of his house. No matter how much they talked

about it or yelled at him, he wouldn't stop. Justin, a
KAV, did not connect riding the bike on that street to
the danger of getting hit. He was impulsive and
enjoyed experiencing life to the fullest. It was difficult
for him to understand the effect of his actions until he
experienced a situation.

Finally, his parents put a replaceable but
treasured object on the street in front of their house
so he could actually see what happened when it was
hit by a car. They chose one of his favorite action
figures. Once Justin saw his action figure flattened
into the pavement by a car, he stopped riding his
bike in the street.

THE KAV & EDUCATION

People with the KAV processing pattern can be a joy to
have in a classroom or training situation. They are
usually very social if they have solid self-esteem, and they
relish sharing their experiences with others. They love to
tell jokes and interesting stories, and they're natural
actors. Group work and hands-on projects are usually
their favorite times in class.

KAVs have difficulty learning from visual material
because that is their weakest processing sense. They will
tend to space out with too much visual work—whether
the material is in print or displayed on a chalkboard,
video, or computer screen. KAVs need to take time out
frequently to rest their eyes; placing them by a window
can help their eyes to relax.

As we mentioned before, KAV processors might have
difficulty organizing their papers and work areas in
conventional ways. In general, a simple organizational
structure is best. For example, many KAVs become confused with a folder for every class. They may do better
with just one folder for all homework that needs to be
completed and one folder for homework that is finished.

KAVs tend to shy away from reading and writing,
since it takes so much effort for them to stay visually
focused. Most KAVs end up rereading material—perhaps
more than once—in order to comprehend it. KAV
students can improve their reading fluency and comprehension if they rock, sway, bounce on a large ball, or

walk while they read. Placing a green transparency over their reading—whether it's in print or on a computer screen—can improve their ability to stay focused and comprehend what they are reading.

People with the KAV processing pattern seem to be the biggest procrastinators of the six patterns. Because they have difficulty planning ahead or envisioning the steps involved in a task, they may become too over-whelmed to even begin. As a result, KAV students may develop poor study habits and a routine of cramming before tests. Although some of them actually work better under the stress of deadlines, cramming doesn't work for most KAVs. They need to have time to experience the information and work with it. Note cards can help KAVs study what they need to know. They can refer to the cards as they move around and use their bodies to imprint the information.

■ *Case Study #18: Ellen's Rocking Chair*

Ellen, a right hemisphere-dominant KAV, always had trouble with tests. She panicked the night before, became even more anxious and confused when she saw the test itself, and could never finish all of the questions within the time allowed.

Ellen knew that what she read didn't seem to stay in her mind, so she figured it was best to just cram all the information into her head the night before a test. By the time she closed the book and went to bed, she usually had a terrific headache and stayed awake all night worrying.

After some training, Ellen started studying for her tests a week ahead of time. She used note cards, looking at them and reading them aloud as she rocked in her rocking chair. Ellen thought it was a crazy idea to rock and talk as she studied her note cards until she saw the pay-off. She was able to complete the next test on time and, in addition, received a grade of "B."

Breaking material down into small units will help KAV processors to handle things better. But they need to learn how to plan ahead as well. Until they do *both* of these things, they will continue to wait until the last minute and then recall little of what they studied. KAVs express their frustration about this with remarks like, "It doesn't matter how hard I study, I never remember it anyway," or, "What's the use of studying? I always forget the information when I take the tests."

Unfortunately, some KAVs become defeated and quit trying to study altogether. Blaming the problem on their forgetfulness, they choose to forget their books and test dates. This is a very common avoidance or survival technique used to cover up a fear of failure. Whenever I ask KAVs if they could remember to bring their books home if I paid them $1,000, they always say, "Sure!" By changing their study and test-taking techniques, many KAVs can dramatically increase their ability to recall information.

If KAVs (or AKVs) could have something in education disappear, it would be written tests. They can become overwhelmed by just seeing the number of questions they have to answer within a limited amount of time. Written pop quizzes can be absolutely terrifying to these individuals.

When KAV learners take a written test, they need to break it into small parts. By covering up the lower part of each page and sliding the cover down as they work, their anxiety will diminish. Another technique that can help is for them to touch the paper as they skim over each test page. This helps them to kinesthetically process the layout of the test.

These techniques can be slightly modified to work with computer-based testing. First, KAV processors should scroll through the entire test to get a feel for how long it is. Touching the screen as they do this can be helpful. (But only if the test isn't using a touch-screen response system; they don't want to record answers at this point!) Then, they need to go back to the top and scroll down through the test, answering the questions as they appear. The important thing is to keep a limited amount of new material showing on the screen at any one time, and to take a quick break every 15-20 minutes.

There is a third approach that helps KAVs perform better on tests, although it breaks with traditional classroom testing models. Anxiety will be lower if KAVs are allowed to use their auditory (Level 2) processing sense to support the kinesthetic. Thus, they will do better if they can read the test out loud or have it read to them.

When making corrections, do it orally. Take them aside and talk about their work while showing it to them. Red marks all over their papers totally defeat most KAVs because they cannot quickly see what is correct in comparison to what is wrong. Since they are Level 3 visual processors, using only visual correction can be very damaging to their self-esteem. On the other hand, oral praise is very good for their ego.

Finally, like those with the KVA processing pattern, when KAVs ask for help they need to have the opportunity to *show* others what they believe they've heard and seen.

THE KAV AT HOME

Living with a KAV can be a lot of fun, though somewhat messy. Don't expect a KAV to notice that you finally straightened the picture in the living room or that you cleared off the clutter on the fireplace mantle. KAVs are more concerned with how a place *feels* rather than how it looks to others. They may have piles and special collections stacked on tables, chairs, and even on the floor in various parts of a room.

You probably won't see them sitting still for hours reading a book or writing letters. They like to listen to music, and they usually love to share jokes and stories with you that they can act out.

They often act on impulse, saying things like, "Let's go for a walk. We can do the dishes later." At the same time, they may forget important dates that you've circled on the calendar if you don't remind them ahead of time.

Most KAVs enjoy social functions with a lot of movement and conversation. At their best moments, KAVs are fun, social beings who enjoy sharing and discussing all the exciting parts of their lives.

PROCESSING PATTERNS? SO WHAT?

Now that you have a better understanding of how individuals learn and process information, you may ask yourself, "So what? What does this mean to me in everyday life?"

"Communication does not begin with being understood, but by understanding others."

— Mary Blakely,
Educator & Author

I believe we can enhance our ability to communicate with one another and create more positive relationships if we take the time to know and understand how each of us learns about life's experiences. I also believe that true communication does not begin with being understood, but by making the effort to understand others. The world around us is a mirror for our growth; by understanding others, we gain knowledge about ourselves. Imagine all the positive changes that could be made in our public and private lives if everyone understood and applied this information to their interactions with others.

For a little fun in bringing this chapter to a close, do the exercise on the next page. It's called *Name That Processing Pattern*.

Resources A and B on pages 194–203 in the Appendix describe teaching and training techniques that are designed to accommodate the different processing patterns discussed in this chapter.

EXERCISE: NAME THAT PROCESSING PATTERN

See if you can identify each individual's processing pattern. (Answers are shown at the bottom of the page.)

1. I like to talk a lot, but I don't like to read or write very much.

2. I really like to ride my bike as fast as I can and feel the wind in my face. But don't ask me to sit and read a book.

3. I love to work with my hands and I like to write poetry. I want to be a surgeon.

4. I really love my graphic design classes, but I have difficulty listening to my teachers' lectures.

5. Don't ask me to give you directions unless I can take you there myself. I have a hard time seeing things before I do them.

6. I get in trouble all the time for talking too much in class. I want to be an actress because I like to experience what it feels like to be someone else.

7. I sit at a desk all day working with details, and I enjoy my job.

8. Don't tell me about the car—let me get inside and feel what it would be like to drive it. If you just tell me about it, I won't buy it.

9. I find school to be really easy. I love to read and write. I probably could do without my gym class, though, since I get frustrated with physical activities.

10. Nothing gets by me. I can even tell you what everyone was wearing yesterday and where they sat in the room. I enjoy sitting for hours just watching people.

Answers: 1 AKV, 2 KAV, 3 KVA or VKA, 4 VKA, 5 KAV, 6 AKV, 7 VAK, 8 KVA, 9 VAK, 10 VAK

CHAPTER 4
SENSORY INTEGRATION
& THE MIND

■ ■ ■

*"Our senses are
so many strings
that are struck
by surrounding objects
and that also frequently
strike themselves."*

⌐ Denis Diderot ⌐
ENCYCLOPEDIST & AUTHOR

In the last two chapters we explored hemispheric dominance and the six basic information processing patterns people use for learning. There is one more element that needs to be added to this mix: sensory integration.

WHAT IS SENSORY INTEGRATION?

Simply stated, **sensory integration (SI) is the ability of the mind to access and process information through both the left and right hemispheres of the brain.** This involves the natural flow of information from one side of the brain to the other through the corpus callosum. In essence, it is the ability of the brain to communicate within itself.

Sensory integration is necessary for optimal learning.

Sensory integration is necessary for optimal learning. We cannot separate the mind and body when we talk about educating the whole person. Many people who have difficulties with learning do not have all of their senses integrated correctly.

There are several possible reasons for this lack of integration. One is that these individuals did not crawl long enough as a child. Crawling is nature's way of helping us to integrate our senses. Simultaneously alternating the arms and legs of our body helps us synthesize neurological information through both the right and left hemispheres of the brain.

Injuries and complications at birth are two other factors that can have a negative impact on sensory integration.

CHECKING SENSORY INTEGRATION

Poor sensory integration affects a surprisingly large amount of functions: small and large muscle movements, handwriting, reading, spelling, memory, and speech. There are many ways to check someone's sensory integration. A few are listed below. Details about each are given in the following paragraphs.

1. Cross-Midline Marching
2. Letter & Number Reversal
3. Paper Spatial Orientation
4. Finger-Thumb Coordination
5. Short-Term & Long-Term Recall

1. CROSS-MIDLINE MARCHING

One simple test of sensory integration is to see if individuals are correctly crossing their midline. As described in chapter 2, imagine a line drawn from the crown of a person's head down between his/her feet. Ask the individual to stand up and copy you as you march in place, touching your *right* hand to your *left* knee.

People who do not have their senses correctly integrated will touch their *right* hand to their *right* knee, thinking that they are copying what you are doing. This means they are functioning from only one side of the brain at that time. In other words, their brains are not sharing information between the left and right hemispheres.

2. LETTER & NUMBER REVERSAL

Another way to check sensory integration is to find out how a person perceives letters and numbers on a page of writing. Because every letter of the alphabet is processed from the right or left, a person with poor sensory integration might see the letters "b" and "d" facing in the same direction. Poor SI is one reason some people reverse their numbers and letters when they read or write.

3. PAPER SPATIAL ORIENTATION

A third check for sensory integration is to find out how an individual perceives, and relates to, the written page as a whole. For example, children who don't have correct SI may only see half of the page when they try to read. Handwriting is also influenced when people do not have their senses fully integrated. They may scrunch up their words around the outside of the margins, since their spatial orientation is processing incorrectly.

4. FINGER-THUMB COORDINATION

A fourth technique for checking whether people have fully integrated senses is to have them lightly press the tip of each finger to their thumb on the same hand. They should be able to do this with both hands when their arms are crossed and uncrossed.

5. SHORT-TERM & LONG-TERM RECALL

For most people, short-term memory is located in the left hemisphere of the brain and long-term memory is located in the right hemisphere. A person with incomplete sensory integration will have short-term recall (left hemisphere) and not long-term recall (right hemisphere), or vice versa, depending on the side of the brain through which they process information.

INCREASING SENSORY INTEGRATION

Once you've established that someone does not have correct sensory integration, what do you do?

There are exercises to help people gain greater SI. Any physical activities involving movements that cross the body's midline are beneficial. This physical effort "forces" one side of the body to share information with the other side.

Swimming, gymnastics, tennis, and golf are all excellent for SI. Juggling scarves and dribbling balls are also good ways to develop sensory integration. In our clinical experience, we have discovered that if a child performs sensory integration exercises like these every morning and night for four to five weeks, there is an improvement in their SI.

Eye tracking exercises will also help establish sensory integration. Individuals should be able to visually follow the eraser on a pencil when you move it in front of their face—whether in a circle, up and down, or back and forth. If they cannot keep their eyes focused on the eraser, they need to practice eye tracking exercises.

In these exercises, people follow an object with their eyes repeatedly in order to strengthen their eye muscles. You can also have them track the beam of a flashlight shining on a wall. In fact, any exercise where they practice crossing their own body's midline will help improve their eye tracking.

To see the effect of correct sensory integration, look at the next case study.

■ *Case Study #19: Pictures Of SI*

This example was taken from the records of a seven-year-old child who did not have correct sensory integration when we started working with him. He had been labeled dyslexic.

The top picture was drawn at the beginning. The bottom picture shows the results of an evaluation conducted five months later. Notice the difference. This child really blossomed after he overcame his sensory integration problems, and his dyslexic label was dropped.

Sensory integration techniques are so helpful that anyone can benefit from doing SI exercises. Colleges and sports teams have incorporated sensory integration exercises into their programs as a "brain boost" before tests and games. This makes sense because both sides of the brain need to communicate information to each other in order to achieve optimal mental and physical performance.

If you would like to learn more about sensory integration techniques, review Dr. Paul Dennison's "Brain Gym®" program. It is listed on page 224 in the Appendix under Educational Kinesiology Foundation.

WHOLE-BRAIN LEARNING

When both sides of the brain are communicating effectively, it is called whole-brain learning. As mentioned previously, peak learning occurs when information is processed through both sides of the brain.

When both sides of the brain are communicating effectively, it is called whole-brain learning.

Rap is popular with many people today because it involves the whole brain. Rap involves words with a continuous beat. Since language is processed in the left hemisphere, and music and rhythm are processed in the right, both hemispheres are processing information when a person raps.

If Rap music—or other songs for that matter—was written in verse form to be memorized without a beat, many people couldn't recall the words. Yet when music or a beat are added to words, whole-brain learning takes place. Many people who can't memorize math facts, the alphabet, or a list will use rhythm or a song for long-term recall. How many adults still rely on the alphabet song to recall their ABCs when they are filing? (See the "Rap Pak" tapes used to help kinesthetic-dominant students learn math facts. They're listed in the Appendix under Resource M on page 228.)

THE BODY—HOME OF OUR FIRST LESSONS

Sensory integration is just one of areas that can be checked to see if a child is ready to learn. Many people believe that abstract thinking requires just our minds. In reality, we learn through our body first. We begin with large muscle movements and then go on to smaller muscles. Internalized thinking happens *after* we learn how to process information through our large and small muscles.

When babies begin kicking their legs and flailing their arms, these are not consciously planned movements. Then one day, they make the connection between their moving feet and their hands; they reach for a toe. Once they understand this fundamental spatial orientation—how their body fits in space and how it moves—they are able to plan conscious actions. They will direct their eyes and manipulate their small and large muscles so they work together to create the action of "hand touches toe." They picture the action mentally, and the body follows automatically. We have all been through this many times—learning how to eat with a spoon, tie our shoes, and catch a ball. Internalized thinking starts with our large and small muscles first.

Reading and writing are also connected to spatial orientation skills and muscle movements. Regardless of the language involved, before individuals can read or write they need to recognize the shapes of letters. Unless they understand space, shape, and form physically, they won't be able to understand how different shapes look or feel.

For instance, to make the letter "S," students need to understand through their body how the movement of an "S" feels. If they have a hard time reading and writing, they may need to go back and learn the movement and feel of letter shapes through their bodies. Ask them to physically demonstrate letters, such as "T," "S," and "P."

> **People who have a hard time reading and writing may need to go back and learn the movement and feel of letter shapes through their bodies.**

Even the mathematical concept of fractions begins with our bodies and minds understanding the concepts of over and under: the numerator is *over* the denominator, and the denominator is *under* the numerator. Check students who are struggling with fractions to make sure they physically understand the concepts of above/over and beneath/under.

LEARNING READINESS & TEETH

In the records of junior high school children I have worked with over the years, I have tracked an unusual statistic: whether or not they lost their teeth before they started school. After reviewing this data, I have come to believe that learning readiness is somehow connected to when we lose our baby teeth.

Although I do not have a neurological explanation for this theory, my records show that children who struggle the most with math and reading appear to have lost their baby teeth long *after* they started school. It may be that the chemical reaction in our brain which triggers the loss of these early teeth prepares our mind to process, integrate, and focus on more information.

Here is a list of some of the characteristics these children show. They often:

- Do not have the eye-hand coordination needed to perform small-muscle tasks, and many do not have the body awareness skills needed for school.
- Are tongue thrusters (i.e., they swallow with their tongues going forward).
- Are unaware that their hands can move separately from their wrists, or that their heads can turn separately from their shoulders.
- Hook their hands around door knobs, instead of turning knobs at the wrist as they grasp them.
- Will sit on their feet when sitting in a chair.
- Have difficulty staying focused on a task.

These children can turn out to be some of our most intelligent learners if we don't squelch their spirits when they are going through their awkward developmental process. Late bloomers take their time, and they have to be tough to survive the growth process in our judgmental society. Yet, the end result is well worth the wait!

I began to pay attention to the link between loss of teeth and learning ability when my youngest son was beginning school. The next case study is his story.

■ Case Study #20: The Late Bloomer's Teeth

My son David struggled with reading from the very beginning and didn't seem to have the body aware-ness he needed before he began school. We even held him back from starting kindergarten, because his attention span was so short he couldn't focus on a full-length cartoon. He was clearly a late bloomer, and his developmental skills were behind the other children in his class.

For example, when his classmates lost their front teeth, David's two front teeth were as solid as cement in his jaw. I will never forget the day he went into the garage and used pliers to pull out his front tooth, determined to be toothless like his friends. There was no way that his tooth was even a little loose, yet he yanked it out. I can only imagine the pain he suffered. His determination to be like his friends was stronger than his fear. Of course, his permanent front tooth didn't come in for a very long time.

The same determination that he had to pull out his tooth carried him through a lot of difficult and frustrating educational experiences involving reading, writing, and spelling. There was even a time when he didn't think he could read. But whatever the challenge, he worked hard and conquered it.

David is a successful businessman today—perhaps because this strong determination to overcome any challenge was tested when he was so young. Although he struggled throughout most of his early elementary years with reading and writing, today he has all the necessary skill, talent, and passion to motivate, lead, and positively influence many people.

Our educational system is based on the belief that age primarily determines a child's readiness to learn. As a result, those who do not fit into what society considers to be a "normal" learning pattern endure frustrations, challenges, and the shame of being labeled in some way as "abnormal." The next section illustrates this problem by examining one of the biggest issues we face in education today—the large number of students being diagnosed with ADD or ADHD.

ADD & ADHD—WHAT DO THE LABELS MEAN?

The telephone calls begin the same way. "Hello. I have an ADD child who needs some help." Or, "Hi, I'm the parent of an ADD child. There's something wrong with his brain that he needs to take drugs for."

After years of working with children who have been labeled with Attention Deficit Disorder or Attention Deficit

Hyperactivity Disorder (and their parents), I'm amazed at how much the public doesn't understand about ADD/ADHD. In my opinion, these labels have become "wastebasket terms" that help us describe and handle the symptoms of overwrought and often forgotten kinesthetic-dominant learners. Symptoms such as daydreaming, fidgeting, restlessness, impulsiveness, and unfinished work can be seen when kinesthetic processors are forced to focus on tasks for long periods of time without moving their bodies. Unfortunately, it can be easier and faster to label students as ADD or ADHD—and even put them on drugs—than to take the time to identify their individual hemispheric dominance, brain processing pattern, and level of sensory integration.

Behaviors similar to ADD/ADHD can be seen in people with hypomania or during the manic phase of bipolar disorder. Also, significant numbers of people experience ADD-type behaviors after they consume a lot of caffeine, sugar, or fast food.

Some outstanding therapists and doctors are aware of this. They thoroughly investigate and consider all of the other possibilities (e.g., environmental allergies, reactions to specific foods, emotional conflicts, sensory integration problems) before they label a patient as ADD/ADHD or administer any type of drug. However, too many adults and children who are Level 1 kinesthetic processors are diagnosed as having ADD or ADHD simply because they have a hard time staying focused on visual or auditory tasks that do not include enough small and large muscle movements. Believe it or not, there are three- and four-year-olds who have been diagnosed with ADD and given prescriptions for drugs to "control" it.

ADD & ADHD—WHO "HAS" IT?

What can life be like for someone with ADD or ADHD symptoms? Imagine yourself in the next case study.

■ *Case Study #21: ADD In The Morning…*

You're wide awake and ready to go in the morning, mentally running through your "to-do" list before you're even out of bed. You start the shower. While waiting for the water to heat up, you start eggs cooking and put toast in the toaster. A friend calls and wonders if he can borrow your guitar. You promise to bring it with you today. You need to find the case for the guitar, so you look in the closet. No guitar, but you find a sock that you've been looking for and decide to put it in the laundry. You see your clean shirts hanging up in the laundry room. The shirt you wanted to wear is dirty and sitting in a large pile of laundry. So you begin a load of laundry. While you're in there, you decide to save yourself some time and put on the clean clothes that are hanging up. But you haven't taken your shower yet, and something smells like it's burning. You run to the kitchen and turn off the stove under your burned eggs. Then you rush to the shower. While you are combing your hair, you remember that you didn't put any detergent in the wash. You dash to the laundry room, but your load is already in the rinse cycle. As you're putting on your clothes, you realize that the detergent is almost gone. You suddenly remember that you went to bed early last night. You want to know if your favorite hockey team won, so you decide to hop in the car and go to the corner store to get some detergent and a newspaper. You grab your coat and the keys hanging just outside the laundry room by the back door. As you slide your

bare feet into your old shoes, you see that your dog is waiting at the door to be let out. While you let the dog out to run in the dog pen, you notice that it seems pretty bright out for so early in the morning. You check your watch. Oh my gosh! You're late! You grab your briefcase and hop in the car, forgetting the guitar, your socks, and the dog. Off you go!

Of course, all of us have days that seem to go like this. But when it happens often or becomes the way we run our lives, this kind of behavior is thought of as being scattered, unfocused, exhausting, and unproductive. It may even be viewed as "abnormal."

It may be that individuals with the symptoms of ADD or ADHD are some of our most intelligent people. As noted previously, they may be Level 1 or Level 2 kinesthetics who, for unknown reasons, have the ability to interact with the environment and process a lot of thoughts rapidly. We know their behavior is not constant or inevitable; it can change under specific conditions. For instance, they are able to stay focused on one thought or task longer if they are emotionally attached to the subject matter or if they use their large or small muscles while working on it.

Thus, it is possible that symptoms identified as typical of ADD and ADHD also emerge when kines-thetic-dominant learners lack the amount of stimula-tion required for their brains to remain focused. The amount of stimulation we receive is determined by the proprioceptors within our large and small muscles and tendons, which constantly send messages to our brain. These messages enable us to know where each part of our body is and how it is moving. When more proprio-ceptor signals reach our brain, the brain is stimulated more; it is easier to stay focused on a task.

People whom we label as ADD or ADHD are almost invariably those who need to touch their environment or move their body in order to process sensory information kinesthetically. If both need this stimulation, what is the difference between the two?

In my opinion, it has to do with the level of stimula-tion required to keep the brain engaged and focused. Individuals diagnosed with Attention Deficit Disorder do not seem to need as much stimulation as those with Attention Deficit Hyperactivity Disorder. The label ADD may actually refer to people who use their small muscles to touch and feel their environment in order to gather information. In the same way, the label ADHD may refer to people who need large-muscle activity or movement to stay focused. Think of those with ADD symptoms as requiring small-muscle movements, and those with ADHD as requiring large-muscle movements

Many children who struggle to sit still for more than 15 or 20 minutes will be calmer and more focused after they run or jump for several minutes. This movement is Mother Nature's way of stimulating the brain. When kinesthetic-dominant children get out of their chairs and use their large muscles for two to five minutes, they are sharper and more task-oriented than when they work straight through on a task for more than 20 minutes.

ADD/ADHD—Diet & Drugs

There is enormous controversy about the importance of diet and how, when, or even whether to use drugs in stabilizing the behavior of those with ADD or ADHD symptoms. I am not going to debate the pros and cons of all this in this book, but simply make some observations.

If you watch carefully, you will notice a marked difference in children when they have had a lot of sugar or are not getting proper nutrition in their diets. Especially during Halloween, Christmas, Easter, and birthdays you may see a drop in their abilities after they have consumed sugar. They may become unsettled, tend to have less patience, and complain of headaches.

Man-made drugs, such as Ritalin, Adderal, Cylert, and Prozac are prescribed for children and adults with ADD or ADHD. Medical research has not come up with a definitive conclusion about the overall effects of such drugs on the brain; I have seen both positive and negative reports regarding their use. However, I personally have some concerns about them.

You may have questions also and might wish to do your own research about drugs currently used for ADD and ADHD. If you do, explore some of the potential alternative remedies. Many of your questions can be answered by looking under topics such as: nutrition and learning disabilities, behavior and nutrition, grades and nutrition, vitamins and minerals, violence and nutrition, nutraceuticals, and homeopathic remedies.

For those people who have ADD or ADHD, some man-made drugs can help if they are administered for a short period of time. However, these drugs should be given only to those who have true ADD or ADHD symptoms, not just "disruptive" kinesthetic processors. They need to be carefully dosed and monitored.

A BRIEF LOOK: THE RESULTS PROJECT

A while ago, I met a wonderful man named Steve Plogg. He tours the country with his program, *I'm O.K.—You're ADD Deficient!* I was so impressed with what he had to say, that I asked him if I could include him in this book.

Steve shares with audiences his story about what it's like to have Attention Deficit Hyperactivity Disorder. He talks about the positive aspects of being ADD or ADHD and explains why he is proud to carry the ADHD label society has given him. Steve considers himself to be a "multiple thought person," meaning his thoughts can shift extraordinarily quickly as he constantly monitors the environment. He can process many different thoughts in rapid succession while working out solutions to problems. Steve has made an incredible personal journey, shifting his point of view about ADHD from something that was a problem to a trait that is an opportunity. In fact, he considers those who aren't ADD or ADHD to be "multiple thought impaired"!

Steve has helped entire school systems to lower or eliminate drugs and violence with his program, called *The Results Project*. His work has shown that a lot of our behavior is connected to what we put into our bodies. *The Results Project* answers the question, "What would happen if schools and businesses offered fresh fruit and vegetables to students and employees instead of highly processed foods, caffeine, and sugar?" (More information about Steve Plogg and his nutritional project is included in the Appendix on page 227.)

IS THERE MORE ADD/ADHD TODAY?

The question is often asked, "Why are so many more people being diagnosed with ADD and ADHD today?" The correct question may actually be, "*Do* we have more people with ADD and ADHD today?"

I have come to believe that the labels ADD and ADHD are being utilized by our society to describe something beyond what those terms originally meant. They are used as a type of shorthand to explain the symptoms kinesthetic-dominant learners have developed as they try to cope with our current lifestyle and educational environment.

Schools originated around farming communities, when people were outside doing chores and using their bodies every day. They even had to use their large muscles to pump water to get a drink. In our current "sit still and think about it" society, children are expected to learn more and learn it more quickly than their parents did. The average classroom today is either Visual-Auditory-Kinesthetic (look, listen, and sit still) or Auditory-Visual-Kinesthetic (listen, look, and sit still).

As we discussed in chapter 3, kinesthetic processors have a difficult time learning effectively unless teachers offer a hands-on curriculum with lots of projects. The sheer volume of information they have to process through their two weakest senses creates high stress, making it even harder for kinesthetic learners to keep up with their Level 1 visual and auditory peers.

Many parents of Level 1 kinesthetic children have shared with me the frustrations of their own educational experiences. As they describe their kinesthetic children—now labeled ADD or ADHD—they also describe how hard school was. They talk about how they couldn't stay focused on their work and how much they hated sitting in their seats all day. Some parents are so relieved that they cry after I finish explaining how their child can learn.

In summary, what variables are contributing to the perceived increase in people developing ADD or ADHD? Here are a few.

When parents discover the best way for their kinesthetic-dominant children to learn, they often make comments like these.

■ "You just explained things I've always thought about myself."

■ "I wish that I had had someone like you to help me when I was my son's age."

■ "All these years I thought there was something wrong with me."

■ "I hated taking all those drugs just so I could learn."

- Children are under greater stress, pushed by a faster-paced lifestyle and increased pressure to perform.
- Students today are learning more than 10 times the information their parents were required to learn. This volume increases with each generation.
- There are new subtle energies surrounding us that influence our physical and mental states, including microwave ovens, televisions, computers, fluorescent lighting, etc.
- More people have poor diets, with a greater intake of chemicals, food additives, sugar, caffeine, and fast food.
- People in general seem to be more susceptible to both known and unknown allergens in food and the environment.
- Individuals raised within the allopathic medical tradition expect "instant cures" and increasingly powerful drugs to handle their concerns. They have difficulty implementing a long-term strategy for health.
- Children from dysfunctional families seem to act out more frequently in an attempt to draw attention and get help with their problems at home.
- In most schools, we don't use effective educational techniques for all learning styles.

Unfortunately, all of these factors—and others—increase as our environment changes and the demands of living in this society accelerate. During the past decade, we have made significant positive changes in awareness concerning the environment, our lifestyle, and our mental and physical health. However, we have a lot more to learn, especially in the areas of drugs and nutrition.

I believe until we begin to look at "who" instead of "what," and offer educational and training programs for each person's processing pattern, many people will continue to suffer. In the meantime, we are suppressing some of our most intelligent and talented individuals, damaging their self-esteem and giving them labels and drugs so they fit into our current instructional and employment structure.

CHAPTER 5
THE HEART–LOVE & FEAR

■ ■ ■

"To love you as I love myself
is to seek to hear you
as I want to be heard
and understand you as
I long to be understood."

~ David Augsburger ~
MEDIEVAL MYSTIC

Ask a group of adults to list any 10 emotions on a flip chart or board, then stand back and observe what they come up with. It is highly predictable: the list will contain from 60 to 80 percent negative emotions.

Although it may not seem like it when we're very busy, our minds hold only one idea at a time. **Therefore, at any given moment you can hold either a positive or a negative thought—but not both.**

Napoleon Hill, the author of *Think and Grow Rich*, writes that 80 percent of our thoughts are negative. To better understand why we do what we do, it is critical that we understand how our minds and bodies are influenced by positive and negative thoughts. In previous chapters we have explored the brain and the mind. Now it's time to take a look at how our emotions are connected with our thoughts and beliefs.

I can recall lying in bed one night at the age of 10 and having an earth-shaking thought: without the color black, we can't know what white is. That's when I also surmised that we need good in order to know bad, happiness to know sadness, and life to know death. Since that time I have continued my personal research about life, and I have expanded that exploration to include love—what it is and what it is not.

THE BASIC EMOTIONS: LOVE & FEAR

> If you trace all other emotions back to their source, love or fear will emerge.

Two fundamental emotional states seem to have the most influence on what we do: love and fear. If you trace all other emotions back to their source, love or fear will emerge.

When people describe what they need help with, the bottom line always seems to be attached to a fear of something. Some of the most common fears are:

- I can't learn.
- I'm too fat.
- I'm not lovable.
- No one likes me.

Ultimately, these fears all stem from the same belief: "I don't think I'm good enough."

Every one of us is searching for true self-acceptance and self-love. It doesn't matter who you are—wealthy or poor, young or old, educated or ignorant, thin or fat. **If you don't believe that you are enough—just as you are—to be loved and valued and respected, then you believe one of two things: (1) you need to change to be enough, or (2) you cannot change and you will never be enough.** The first carries the burden of frustration, shame, and guilt. The second carries the burden of failure and hopelessness. If you tell yourself, "I need to be smarter, stronger, thinner, prettier, and/or more... whatever," then at some level you don't believe you are enough. I am convinced the main message that all people need to hear and believe is, "You already are and always will be enough, just as you are!"

LOVING OURSELVES

What does it mean to love yourself? Self-love is not egotistical or narcissistic. It is knowing deep inside that you are enough—i.e., that you have value and worth, that you are lovable. Mature self-love is understanding and responding to your own truth, and giving yourself what supports your life. When you deny yourself things that are nurturing, you are starving your soul.

> You already are and always will be enough, just as you are!

We all say that we love a child, we love nature, or we love music. Yet, can we honestly say that we love ourselves? This seems to be the hardest thing to do. **When we don't believe we are enough**—that we are worthy to be respected and loved—**we experience unhappy circumstances in which we feel lonely and empty.**

People who don't trust other people usually don't trust themselves. Until we learn to trust and love ourselves as the wonderful creation that we are, we can't truly know love.

LOVING OTHERS

There are all types of emotions connected to others that are labeled as love. Love can be experienced between

> **"Love is a verb."**
>
> — Clare Boothe Luce,
>   Diplomat & Author

parents and children, siblings, friends, partners, and even with treasured pets. Whatever the relationship may be, true love is unconditional. It is given and received freely, without demands and expectations attached. Love is a constant within each of us—the essence of our very being that is reflected back through others.

What is the first step to loving someone or something else? It starts within yourself. The first step to knowing love is to acknowledge your own thoughts and feelings. If you love someone, admit it to yourself. This can be very difficult. You may be so afraid of being hurt that you don't want to admit your love to yourself, much less to someone else. This is one way many people miss out on experiencing a loving relationship.

At some point you may decide to tell someone how you feel. Opening yourself up and expressing your feelings of love to another person can be a scary experience, especially if you believe that you are risking rejection. But love isn't about being loved in return. It's about loving someone or something just because you do. Whether or not you tell other people that you love them isn't as important as accepting and owning your feelings of love. **If you deny your love for anything or anyone in life, you are imprisoning your "self,"** the very essence of who you are.

Why do we equate love with ownership? Expressions like, "I can't live without you," and "Without you I am nothing," are found in many popular songs. Just because we love someone doesn't mean that we need to own him/her. In fact, love based on a desire to own or control another person is not love. It is actually a feeling attached to needs generated by the fear of not being enough.

I believe that true love in a partnership occurs when both individuals love themselves as well as each other. When you love yourself well, you are secure within yourself. You do not need to depend on other people for validation, so you don't need to try to control them.

Why we love can be the subject of an entire book by itself. You will experience many feelings that you will label as love in your life, but they will always reflect the amount of love you have for yourself. We all want to be loved and know that we are enough. Most people spend a lifetime trying to achieve this.

> "You do not need to be loved,
> Not at the cost of yourself...
> Of all the people you will know in a lifetime,
> you are the only one you will never leave or lose."
>
> — Jo Courlet

FEAR: THE REACTIVE BRAIN

To understand the power of fear in our lives, we need to start with human physiology. At the most fundamental level, fear begins in our bodies.

Our brain is a wonderful organ, developed to monitor our needs and take care of us. One area of the brain—called the reptilian, primitive, or reactive brain—is responsible for physical regulation and staying alive. **Our reactive brain cares about one thing: survival.**

Have you ever watched a cornered animal that sees no escape? It will fight back, even if it means death. Our bodies are structured in the same way; we also will go into "fight or flight" mode in order to survive.

Whenever you are afraid, your reactive brain automatically sends signals throughout your body, helping you to prepare for "fight or flight." The actual physiological processes are incredibly complex and, for the most part, not under conscious control. Adrenaline kicks in, your heart beats faster, your hands begin to sweat, your breathing increases, and your blood pressure goes up. This enables you to fight or escape from whatever you perceive to be a threat.

Some researchers believe that our bodies know we are afraid about eight seconds before this registers in our conscious mind. If this is true, our reactive brain has set all of these physiological responses in motion before we are even aware that we're afraid of something.

When your primitive brain is in charge, you are likely to react overtly to fear. For example, you may hit someone before you stop to think. Or you may actually run away, perhaps running into even more danger as you are trying to escape and survive. This response to fear is absolutely critical to survival when you are faced with physical danger. Without it, you could be seriously injured or die.

Yet, there are many times when we need to temper our reactions and see our fear for what it is. Our reactive brain doesn't judge the degree or appropriateness of our fear, so it doesn't matter if we are being chased by a tiger or if we are asked to sing the national anthem in front of a group. If we think we might not survive the experience or that we don't have the resources to meet the challenge, our primitive brain sounds the "fight or flight" bells.

This creates a problem. If our bodies react before we even know we're afraid, how can we change our instinctive response?

To keep your reactive brain from controlling you, you simply need to acknowledge your fear. Once you say to yourself (silently or out loud), "I'm afraid," your primitive/reactive brain has done its job. It raised the alarm and prepared your body to react.

Now your higher brain functions can take over, and things will start to settle. Your heartbeat and breathing will slow down, and your blood pressure will fall. Once this happens, you can choose how to respond to a threatening situation. As long as you are being controlled by your body's reactions, you are no different than an animal living on its survival instinct. Yet, by acknowledging your fear and using your higher brain functions to deal with what is occurring, you can *choose* to fight, flee, or understand and face your fear.

FEAR & CONTROL

Whenever we see ourselves as not being enough or having enough, we go into fear mode.	What does this have to do with the mind/body connection and our beliefs?
	Whenever we see ourselves as not being enough or having enough,

we go into fear mode. To understand how these thoughts can affect our minds and bodies, it is necessary to see how these thoughts connect to the belief, "I am not enough."

If you agree that the two major emotions in life are love and fear, then any emotion not based on love must be based on fear. Fear underlies emotions like jealousy, anger, and hate. Anger is always a symptom of fear—the fear of not being able to cope, of not being enough.

Fear arises any time we feel like we are losing—or have already lost—control of some aspect of our lives. Anger emerges from this as a symptom of fear. In other words, when we feel angry we are really afraid of not being in control in some way. We question whether or not we will survive.

We can fall into the victim role when we are afraid that we are losing control. One of the first things we might say when we are presented with one of life's challenges is, **"Why me?"** I once heard a priest consoling a patient who was saying those very words. The priest replied, **"Why not you?"** He was a wise priest. He empowered this patient by not allowing him to be victimized by his illness or his fear.

We also project our anger onto those people or things that we believe control us. Once you understand this dynamic about fear and control, you will never be an unaware victim again. Of course, you may be temporarily victimized in a particular situation, such as a robbery or mugging. But this is different from taking on the role of

Before I work with anyone who has cancer I ask them, "Do you have cancer or does cancer have you?" If they reply that they have cancer, then I may be able to help them. If they reply, "Cancer has me," I cannot help them.

The difference is fundamental to healing. If you have cancer, it is a guest in your house. You can ask it to leave. If cancer has you, it has taken over your house, and you can't ask it to leave. Who is in control, the disease or you?

A man with cancer once invited me to his home. When I asked him this question, he said with conviction, "Cancer has me." I told him that unless he changed his belief about who was in control of the cancer, I couldn't help him.

He had already decided who would leave. He died several weeks later.

victim. You may still choose to be a victim, but deep inside you will know that you really aren't.

I experienced this myself when I had to deal with the IRS once. I teach this material every day, yet I found myself actually looking up at the sky and saying, "Leave me alone!" As if the IRS was running my life! Of course, right after I heard myself say these words, I knew I had fallen into victim mode. I quickly changed my point of view. But for that short amount of time, I gave the IRS control of my life. When my higher brain functions finally took over, I realized that my fear of not having enough was right in front of my face; it was ridiculous to give the IRS so much power over me.

We should note one other thing about fear and anger. Many people ask if anger is always negative or bad. In my opinion, no. I believe that the anger which arises from fear is an expression of pain. And pain triggers change.

Anger can be very helpful for a short amount of time. It can be the "kick in the pants" that gives us the determination and energy to change. But long-term anger can damage our health and well-being. It can keep us tied to someone or something, blocking us from moving forward. When this happens, the choice to stay angry is feeding a belief of some kind. For example, we may be projecting anger onto another person instead of owning up to a bigger fear within ourselves.

FEAR & THE REACTIVE BRAIN AT HOME

As a rule of thumb, the lower our self-esteem, the more sensitive we are to potentially negative situations, and the faster our reactive brain responds to perceived threats.

For example, child abuse often occurs when an adult's reactive brain is triggered by a person or situation in which they feel out of control, unworthy, unloved, or unable to cope. The adult may lash out at a child because he/she is smaller and happens to be the nearest target. This leads the child to feel afraid, unloved, and "not enough." Unless abused children receive help in dealing with their fear and anger, they may carry their emotional wounds into their lives as adults. Then the pattern of abuse is repeated in yet another generation.

In the next case study, we look at how fear, control, and the reactive brain affect our everyday life.

■ *Case Study #22: Betty, Jim & The Garage*

One winter morning, Betty asked her teenage son, Jim, to clean out the garage so she could use it for her car. She was frustrated with having to get up early every morning and clean the snow off her car before she went to work. Jim promised he would. Betty left, expecting it to be done when she got home that afternoon.

In spite of an early start, Betty was late for work because the roads were worse than usual. Warned that she would be fired if she came in that late again, Betty worried all day that she might lose her job. She was still afraid and angry when she headed home.

In the meantime, Jim had a bad day at school. It seemed as if everything went wrong. He even flunked a math test that he thought he would easily pass. All he wanted to do was go home, sit down in a quiet space, and drink a soda.

When Betty came home and saw Jim sitting on the sofa, she pounced on him. "Don't you even think about going out or talking to your friends on the phone until you clean up the garage. I'm tired of your selfishness." Jim, tired and withdrawn, rolled his eyes and muttered, "Whatever." Betty then yelled, "Don't you roll your eyes at me. You are grounded. Go to your room!"

What is really going on in this picture? First, Betty is very upset with Jim for not cleaning the garage. She feels that he is taking advantage of her and being disrespectful. To top it off, she believes her son is lazy and that this is causing her to have problems with her job.

When she walks through the door at the end of the day, Betty is already afraid and angry from work. Then, when she sees Jim on the sofa, her reactive brain takes over. In reality, Betty is afraid that she has lost parental control; this gets expressed as anger. Jim rolls his eyes at his mother as if he doesn't care. He feels she is being disrespectful toward him, and this is his reactive way of responding to that. After Betty sees Jim roll his eyes at her, her reactive state of mind says, "That's disrespectful.

A good parent raises her son to show respect. You must be a terrible parent to let your child treat you this way." This cycle of fear and anger escalates quickly, ending when Betty feels that she only has one way to take back parental control: by grounding Jim.

This short scene illustrates how quickly we can fall into fear and let our reactive brain take charge. What might happen if Betty and Jim understood the dynamics of fear, anger, and control? Let's replay the same scene with that awareness on both sides.

■ *Betty, Jim & The Garage continued...*

Jim is tired and upset about school. As before, he comes home and sits down for a few minutes to drink a soda. Betty is afraid and angry about work. When she comes home and sees him on the sofa, she confronts him with the same remarks.

However, Jim understands why his mother is angry. He knows that he deserves the reprimand and that he will have to clean the garage. His mother is right; he promised he would do it. Still thirsty and tired, he says, "OK, I hear you, but can I finish my soda first?"

Betty, expecting her buttons to be pushed, feels heard and treated with respect instead. Her anger dissipates as her fear of not being a good parent melts away. She says to herself, "He did just get home from school. He looks exhausted. I remember how much I used to want to just come home and relax." After quickly analyzing her son's frame of mind, Betty replies in a calmer voice, "OK, you can have some time to unwind, but I still expect you to clean the garage before you start anything else." The result? Betty gets the garage cleaned, and Jim doesn't get grounded. Both retain their sense of self-worth and dignity. And both are in control, no longer operating out of the reactive brain.

FEAR & THE REACTIVE BRAIN IN THE WORKPLACE

How does fear affect our behavior at work? Although our conduct may be under tighter control at work than in our personal lives, the dynamics of fear, anger, and control play out in the same manner.

For example, some people who are very good employees may not read or do math very well. They go to work every day afraid that someone may discover their "secret." If their boss forces them to read or work with numbers in front of other employees, they may become very angry for no apparent reason. They will create a scene or become ill. Losing one's temper, procrastination, illness, and tardiness are all responses to fear in these situations.

The next case study explores a typical situation in a company.

■ *Case Study #23: Bob & Tom*

> *Bob is a middle manager in the XYZ Products Company. One day he is walking back to his office after a meeting in which he learned that his lack of diligence caused the company to suffer a setback. He sees Tom, one of his employees, talking casually to a group of other staff members about an upcoming Little League baseball game.*
>
> *Bob stops and explodes at Tom. He calls Tom lazy and tells him to get back to work or he'll be fired. He yells, "Get back to work now!" Tom, stunned and furious, yells back, "Hey I'm not the only one standing here talking." He*  *then turns his back on Bob and continues to talk with the other employees. Bob fires Tom on the spot.*

Bob's damaged self-esteem, seriously undercut by his own job problems, causes much of this interaction. (Remember, the lower a person's self-esteem, the quicker the reactive brain steps in to take control.) But Tom has problems too. Let's look at the interaction to see how fear is controlling both of them.

Any boss who belittles someone in front of other employees is trying to demonstrate or recover power and control. When a boss intimidates his employees and creates fear, he is actually afraid that he doesn't have control of the situation.

In this case study, Bob has just left a meeting where he feels he lost control in a situation that negatively affected his company. He's afraid and angry. When Bob sees Tom talking with the other employees, he goes immediately into his reactive brain. He sees an employee wasting time, and he knows it is his job to keep control of the workplace. Bob believes that he needs to take control back, so he yells at Tom and belittles him.

Tom has always felt like a victim, believing that life is constantly dumping on him. His teachers never liked him and he knows that his boss feels the same way. He's always the one they point the finger at, regardless of whether he's at fault or not. So Tom is very sensitive to Bob's behavior and words. When Tom sees Bob walking up, he knows Bob is angry. Tom is already prepared for the worst when Bob starts yelling at him. Afraid, angry, and embarrassed, Tom yells back, "Hey, I'm not the only one standing here talking." He then continues to talk in order to show his boss and colleagues that he won't be intimidated and belittled in front of others. As a result, Tom gets fired.

How might the scene be different if Bob understood the dynamics of fear, anger, and control?

■ *Bob & Tom continued...*

> *As Bob walks down the hallway after the meeting, he's upset with himself for losing control. He's temporarily operating out of his reactive brain. When Bob sees Tom talking, his blood pressure goes up immediately. But he understands where his anger comes from, admits to himself that he's angry, and knows that he'd like to project it onto someone else. Bob says to himself, "That man is goofing off again and pulling everyone else with him. He's wasting time and money. I need to get him back on the job."*
>
> *Instead of belittling Tom, Bob calls him over and takes him away from the group. Tom is tense and afraid, expecting to be yelled at since he believes that he's always the victim. Bob talks quietly with Tom. "I know that you need to take breaks every now and*

then, but I'm counting on you to help me keep everyone focused on their work. I know they look up to you and will follow your lead."

In this situation, Tom's victim trigger is diffused. Because Bob treated him with respect and didn't try to control him, Tom feels like a team player. He returns to work with the feeling that he is respected and appreciated. Tom doesn't get fired, and Bob stays "in control."

Whether you are dealing with situations at work or in your personal life, the dynamic around fear, anger, and control is the same: **if you have to work hard to keep control, you've never had control.**

Being "in control" in its best sense means that you empower others and help to direct or facilitate a positive, ongoing flow of energy throughout the group. **When you struggle to maintain control by being a "controller," you are acting from the fear that you won't be able to control the situations in which you find yourself.** Ironically, a controlling person is never actually in control.

> Ironically, a controlling person is never actually in control.

FEAR & LEARNING

When teenagers are not turning in their homework or are choosing to skip class, they are most likely operating out of fear. For example, when a student is sitting in a math class where he feels he can't be successful, and the teacher calls on him to answer a problem, he immediately goes into fear mode. His brain jumps into a reactive state. It doesn't matter that it's "just" a math teacher asking a question; anything or anyone can trigger fear if you think you're not good enough and that someone or something is in control of you.

To understand how fear affects learning, consider the two processing patterns discussed earlier in chapter 3. Remember how important it is for KVA and KAV learners to touch or move in their environment so they can imprint information into long-term memory?

Now imagine them in a classroom that requires them to listen to an hour-long lecture or to read without including their kinesthetic sense. They will experience a lot of frustration. The KAVs won't recall what they read and will have a hard time staying focused on visual work. The KVAs won't recall what the teacher said. Both will struggle and consider the class boring—an indication that they aren't imprinting the information being taught. This is often the first step before they zone out or daydream.

In addition, KAVs and KVAs may develop a fear of failure in any classes that focus on their weakest (Level 3) processing sense. To cope with this fear, they may choose to avoid doing the work in these classes by skipping lessons, not doing their homework, forgetting their books, or not handing in assignments.

Since kinesthetic-dominant processors feel their emotions through their bodies, they are often struggling to deal with their fear on the inside even though they appear to be calm externally. Some kinesthetics will avoid any uncomfortable situation. They will develop stomach aches, skip school, misbehave so they're sent to the principal's office, or decide to just disappear for awhile. They may become very proficient at getting out of classes, knowing precisely which buttons to push in each of their teachers.

> **...students who believe that they are stupid would rather look "bad" than stupid to their peers.**

Regardless of their dominant processing style, students who believe that they are stupid would rather look "bad" than stupid to their peers. They may purposefully get into trouble in order to get out of a classroom in which they experience fear and failure.

CHOOSING TO FAIL

People will go through incredible mental contortions to feel safe, maintain their self-esteem, and keep their fear under control. Although it seems illogical, choosing to fail can be one way to achieve this.

For example, many students will procrastinate when it comes to studying for a test. When they are asked, "Would you study if you received some money for doing it?," they usually agree that they would. The reward would be worth the risk of studying and still failing the test. Yet, without a reward or positive reason to risk failure, they will do whatever they have to in order to avoid a test that *might prove* they are a failure. In other words, by not studying **they choose to fail rather than be failed.**

I believe there are four major reasons people of all ages choose to fail. They are all based upon fear.

REASON #1: FEAR OF NOT MEASURING UP TO EXPECTATIONS
"If I give it my best and do well, then they will expect me to do it all the time."

This individual is afraid of not measuring up to another person's expectations and doesn't want to be judged. Many bright individuals appear to be lazy due to this fear.

REASON #2: FEAR OF INCOMPETENCE
"If I give it my best and I still don't do well, then I have to live with the fact that I can't do this. I'd rather not take the risk, or I'd rather do just enough to get by. Then I'll never know."

People who fail for this reason don't believe in their ability to do well. They also may feel they can't live with themselves if they try something and don't succeed.

REASON #3: FEAR OF EXPERIENCING FAILURE
"You can't make me succeed. I really don't care if I fail. This is stupid. You don't know what you're talking about."

These people want to feel safe; they will insulate themselves from fear and pain by using control. When they shut down, project their fears onto someone else, and blame that person, they feel safe and in control.

REASON #4: BELIEF THAT THEY ARE A FAILURE
"I'll just fail anyway; you'll see." "See, I told you I'd blow it."

These individuals believe that they are failures. To maintain this belief, they need to convince others that they are right about this belief.

TECHNIQUES FOR CONTROLLING FEAR

Fear is uncomfortable. As human beings, we have many types of behavior for controlling it. And, as we've seen, not all of them are productive. Here are a few more of the techniques we use for controlling our fears.

We put another person down in order to pull ourselves up.

Whenever a person demeans or belittles someone else, the motivation almost always comes from a fear of not being enough. We put another person down in order to pull ourselves up. Gossiping about another person begins with low self-esteem. If you catch yourself criticizing another person, take a close look in the mirror. Those things that irritate us most about another are often the same things that we're afraid of in ourselves. By examining our gossip or judgmental comments, we can learn about ourselves.

The acts of giving and receiving can also be used to control someone when we are afraid of losing control. Giving and receiving are the same; they both require an open hand. You can't do one without the other. Giving is receiving. In order to receive something, you must also be willing to give. And in order to give, you must be open to receiving.

Giving or receiving to the extreme can be based on a fear of not being or having enough. People who only give in order to receive are attaching an expectation to their giving—that they will get something in return. Some individuals choose to receive or take from others without giving anything back. Still others may always give, never allowing themselves to receive. All of these attitudes toward giving and receiving ultimately relate to control. When we wish to control, we will offer something or take it away.

Bribery and punishment are common in some families or institutions where there is fear of losing control. If you want to see a classic case of control using bribery and punishment, visit a child photographer's booth at the mall. Especially during holidays, there are many control games that go on between parents and the children they want to "smile for the camera." While one child can almost name her price for that smile, another will be scolded or even spanked for not cooperating.

POWER TAKERS/CONTROLLERS

Have you ever left work with a neck ache or a headache that appears to have come from nowhere? Do you ever feel totally drained after being with a certain person? More than likely, you have been involved with a power taker. Power takers can be anything or anyone we allow to take our energy from us. Even a puppy who rules the house can be an energy taker if you feel you've lost your control over him.

We may become power takers/controllers whenever we feel we're not adequate or believe we don't have enough for ourselves. To understand how the subconscious mind deals with power, imagine that we all have tanks strapped on our backs that are similar to divers' oxygen tanks. These tanks supply us with the power we need to survive. How would you feel if someone tapped into your supply and took some of your power? If it meant your survival, you would try to get it back and refill your tank.

Of course, this is just an analogy. But it does have some truth to it. Even though we have an unlimited supply of personal power available to us, we often forget that. We will give away our own power or take someone else's power, depending on what we think we need in order to survive.

Energy Giver   Energy Taker

Energy/Power Loss

We all take power from others at one time or another; that is just part of being human. So it is helpful to know that there are patterns to how we become power takers/controllers. The adults who raised us taught us how to take someone's power in the same way they were taught to take power. You can see how your parents taught you to take someone's power by identifying the major ways you take someone's power. You are likely to teach your children those same methods.

There are two major ways in which we take each other's power: passively and aggressively. Passive power takers/controllers play on your sympathy and vulnerabilities. They pull you in, emotionally seducing you into helping them. On the other hand, aggressive energy takers/controllers directly take your energy by threatening you emotionally or physically in order to pull you into their power.

HOW WE TAKE POWER FROM OTHERS

There are four ways we take power from others.*

1. THE BULLIES
This is the most aggressive method for taking power. It is overt, direct, and intimidating. These people belittle you and attack your self-esteem. They try to overpower you with physical or emotional abuse to get you to give up your power.

2. THE ACCUSERS
This method is aggressive but less direct than that of the bullies. Accusers question you in order to criticize or judge you. As you try to answer their questions, you become self-conscious. You begin to think the Accuser's thoughts and worry that you will do something wrong unless you please him/her. Accusers take your power by manipulating you to think their way.

3. THE SHIELDERS
This passive method for taking power creates a wall between people. Shielders demonstrate the "I could care

---

* Inspired by and partially adapted from James Redfield's book, *The Celestine Vision*.[5]

less" attitude. They set themselves apart from you by putting up walls, with the hope that you will bring them out. This is the "silent treatment" method.

4. THE WHINERS

This is the second passive method for taking power. These people play the martyr game; they get power and attention by making others feel guilty or sorry for them. Whiners make you believe that they will fail or not survive unless you help them. You feel like you can never do enough for these people.

POWER TAKER/CONTROLLER INTERACTIONS

These four methods or types of power manipulation do not operate in a vacuum. They feed off of and interact with each other. Bullies create another Bully or a Whiner. Accusers create another Accuser or a Shielder. In turn, a Whiner may create a Bully, and a Shielder may generate an Accuser. The next two case studies illustrate this process.

■ *Case Study #24: The Bully & The Whiner*

Janice lived with an alcoholic husband who controlled her with his physical strength by slapping her around. (Bully) *Usually Janice took the blame for his behavior, saying, "Please don't hurt me. I promise I'll be a better wife. Just don't leave me."* (Whiner)

Then one day she'd finally had enough. She became strong and angry enough to stand up to him, saying, "I'm leaving you. I don't know why I stayed as long as I did. You aren't worth my time and trouble. You don't deserve me. You are the sorriest, stupidest excuse of a man I've ever seen." (Bully)

When her husband feared that he could no longer control her, he begged her to stay. He sobbed as he blurted out his words. "I'm sorry. I didn't mean to hurt you. I don't know why I did it. I won't hurt you again, I promise. I don't know why you put up with me. You're right. I'm not worth it. I don't deserve you. I need you. Don't leave me now. I can't make it without you." (Whiner)

In cases of abuse, the victim may finally stand up to a Bully by temporarily taking on the guise of a Bully in order to get out of an unhealthy relationship.

But a relationship doesn't have to be abusive for this same switch in roles to occur. Read the following case study involving an Accuser and a Shielder.

■ *Case Study #25: The Accuser & The Shielder*

Tom's father, Ray, was a very controlling man. He was highly intelligent and taught at the local university. To Tom, it seemed like he could never please his father. Ray was always trying to get Tom to see life his way.

One day Tom told his father that he wanted to pursue an acting career. Ray responded predictably. "What would you want to go into acting for? You don't think you can live off an actor's salary, do you? If you follow my advice and go to college and pursue a decent career, you'll make something of yourself that your mother and I can be proud of. Don't you think we deserve a son who can stand on his own two feet someday? Acting won't get you there." (Accuser)

Tom was hurt and angry. He shot back, "You think you know everything, don't you? I've got news for you. You don't. Where do you get off playing god in everyone's life anyway?" (Accuser)

Ray believed he was losing control of Tom for good, but he was so afraid and angry that he couldn't think how to respond. He said the first thing that popped into his head. "This conversation is over. I have nothing more to say to you. You're on your own. Close the door on your way out." (Shielder) *As Tom walked out of the room, he slammed the door. He didn't speak to his father for the rest of the day.* (Shielder)

Do you understand your own primary power taker/ controller pattern? Do you recognize how other people in your life take power from you? Before you finish this chapter, take a few minutes with the next exercise, "Identify the Power Takers."

Then, when you are ready to explore this in more

detail, turn to the two exercises on pages 204–207 in the Appendix of this book. One exercise will help you identify the power takers in your life; the second will help you see how much of yourself you give away to others.

EXERCISE: IDENTIFY THE POWER TAKERS

Can you identify the four methods of taking power in the statements below? Put a letter in the space beside the question—A for Accuser, B for Bully, S for Shielder, and W for Whiner. The answers are at the bottom of the page.

____ 1. "Who cares? I don't need it. It doesn't bother me."

____ 2. "My foreman has it in for me."

____ 3. "When I think you can handle it, I'll tell you. You have a long way to go."

____ 4. "That teacher doesn't like me."

____ 5. "No way am I going to let you have a checking account. You can't even add simple numbers!"

____ 6. "What were you thinking? Who told you that you could make that decision? Did it ever occur to you that you don't have enough experience?"

____ 7. "I do so much for you and this is the thanks I get?"

____ 8. "Did I say that I wanted your participation? Did anyone ask for your opinion?"

____ 9. "You must not love me or you would take me with you."

____ 10. "I don't care. I didn't want to go anyway."

FACING FEAR

When facing fear, it is helpful to remember that you are in control—even when it doesn't feel that way.

I was terrified when I first learned to ski because I wasn't very good at stopping. Then I remembered that I could just sit down when I needed to stop. Whew! After I figured out how I could still be in control and survive no matter what happened, my fear left.

Your power of imagination can help you deal with your fears effectively. Once you identify a fear, you can mentally design various ways for handling it. By doing this, you can prepare yourself for the worst-case scenario—like going over a cliff, or somersaulting down a hill, or getting caught in an avalanche while skiing! As long as you don't stay focused on the worst outcome, this technique can be very beneficial. It will help you take back control mentally and feel safe.

Another technique that can help you handle fear is to ask yourself, "When I compare this to the big picture of life, how important is it in the whole scheme of things?" Most of the time, you will see that your fear is way out of proportion to the situation's true importance in your life.

Whether in a school, a business, or a social organization, people want to understand fear and how it controls them. Everyone can relate to fear. When individuals understand how they create their fears, they are able to consciously take back control of their lives.

FEAR: A SUMMARY

- Fear is based on a belief that, in some way, you are not enough.

- You create fear whenever you feel your control is being taken away.

- Your reactive brain is in control when you are in fear mode.

- When you are afraid, you go into a "fight or flight" pattern.

- To get out of your fear, you must first admit that you are afraid; validate your feelings.

- You can process fear through your higher-level brain functions only after you acknowledge your fear.

- Fear is your biggest block in life.

- It is important for you to know what triggers fear in yourself and what you do to control it.

- When you lose control, you try to become a controller.

- You learn from the adults who raised you how to take power from another.

- You know how to take another person's power, and you have already taught someone else how to take power.

- You will use each of the four power-taking methods to get back control at some time in your life.

- When you understand that you are enough, you don't need to take power or energy from other people.

In the next chapter, we explore the topic of beliefs. Our beliefs help create our fears and shape the methods we use when we try to control situations. This is the key to understanding why we do what we do.

CHAPTER 6
BELIEFS

■ ■ ■

"Man is what he believes."

⌒ Anton Chekhov ⌒
PHYSICIAN & AUTHOR

You experience what you believe.

You experience what you believe. This is probably the most important concept in this book to understand.

HOW BELIEFS ARE LEARNED

By age three, you developed a set of beliefs that established how your needs could be met. Let's say that every time you hurt yourself, your mother gave you a cookie to help you feel better. This action taught you, unintentionally, to believe that cookies take away pain. You now gorge yourself on cookies any time you feel you've been hurt.

Perhaps you were born into a large or busy family where your needs were not met unless you cried loudly enough for someone to hear you. Now, as an adult, you may believe that you need to make a fuss to be sure your needs are met. Your belief may be, "If I don't make a fuss, I won't survive."

You accepted these and many other beliefs as true long before you were able to think them through for yourself. **Many of the beliefs you have today are not "yours."** Instead, they have been passed on from the adults who raised you or other adults who had a significant influence on your life.

For example, how many times have you heard, "Money doesn't grow on trees," or "When life gives you lemons, make lemonade." Each of these may have influenced how you approach life.

The statement about money and trees usually is meant to get across the idea of scarcity—that there is not enough money to go around. If you often heard statements like this, you may have developed the belief that there will never be enough money; it will run out.

A good way for you to check what you believe about money is to blindly reach into your wallet or purse during the year-end holidays and give a Salvation Army bell ringer whatever bill your hand pulls out. It could be a $50 or a $1 bill. What is your intention? Watch how you react to what you pull out.

Money has little intrinsic value. It is a physical representation of the value of a certain amount of energy, so it only has value when we (and others) give it importance. What you intend to give is based on your beliefs about giving, not just on what you feel you can give. If you believe it is appropriate to give to others and also believe in abundance, the amount you pull out won't matter because you know there will always be enough to share. If you intend to give your smallest coin, your belief might be, "I can only give a little because I may not always have enough money." Think back to the last time you saw bell ringers standing outside a store. Did you pass them by, reach inside your pocket for some small change, or reach into your wallet? Of more importance, what does your action say about what you believe?

My mother always said, "When life gives you lemons, make lemonade." I thought that was a great statement to live by until I realized that the statement tells you to expect lemons in life!

Of course, the reality is that we all seem to get some lemons in our lives. But if it is true that what we focus on becomes our experience, then what would life be like if we didn't focus on what we intend to do when we get lemons? What if we were taught instead, "When life gives you bowls of cherries," (i.e., abundance) "make cherry pies and share them with others"? It certainly isn't wrong to make lemonade out of lemons when that's appropriate. It's a matter of focus. Do you prefer to think in terms of lemons or cherries? Personally, I prefer to focus on receiving bowls of cherries in my life!

We are often unaware how deeply our collective beliefs are ingrained within us and how strongly they influence us. I work with many fathers and sons who are struggling with the effects from one belief in particular: "Real men don't cry." This belief has caused many boys and men to be emotionally crippled and incapable of

Many of your experiences today are actually being generated from outdated beliefs that you accepted when you were young.

expressing their feelings. It has also added a great deal of stress in their relationships.

What have your family and close friends said to you about your body, money, religion, love, relationships, neighbors, etc.? Many of your experiences today are actually being generated from outdated beliefs that you accepted when you were young.

IDENTIFYING YOUR BELIEFS

Here is a paper-and-pencil exercise that can help you identify your core beliefs. Write down as a phrase or a sentence the first thought that comes into your mind. Don't judge your thought, just get it on paper. Then, at the end of that phrase, write the question, "Why?" Think about what the answer might be, write down that thought, and again put the question, "Why?" at the end of the phrase. Keep writing answers and asking yourself, "why" until you can't give another answer.

The series of statements below shows how this process works.

I am never organized.
Why?
Everything is always a mess around me.
Why?
I never have the time to pick things up.
Why?
I'm too busy to be organized.
Why?
I can't be both busy and organized.
Why?
Because there's too much for me to handle.
Why?
Because I'm always too busy to take care of things.
Why?
Because I choose to be busy.
Why?
Because I don't take time for myself.
Why?

Because others come first.

Why?

Because they are more important than I am.

Why?

Because they count on me.

Why?

Because I'm the only one that can be counted on.

Why?

Because I never let anyone down.

Why?

Because I don't want them to be upset with me.

Why?

Because I want to keep everyone happy.

Why?

Because then I feel good about myself.

Why?

Because if I help people, I feel good.

Why?

Because then I feel like I'm needed.

Why?

Because I need to be needed.

Why?

Because when I'm needed, I feel like I'm enough.

The core belief this exercise revealed is, "When I'm needed, I feel like I'm enough." This may seem to be totally unrelated to the first statement, "I am never organized," but the connection is clear once you've read the sequence of beliefs in between. Underneath each of your completed phrases is the motivating belief of that particular thought.

Now it's your turn to experiment with this discovery exercise. What do you believe when you are given the opening statement, "My life is…"? Turn to the next page.

EXERCISE: IDENTIFYING YOUR LIFE BELIEFS

Finish the statement, "My life is..." with whatever first comes to mind. Don't think about it too long. Answer the question, "Why?" with another statement. If you need more space, use additional pieces of paper. Keep going until you can't give another answer.

My life is _____

Why? _____

Why? _____

Why? _____

Why? _____

Why? _____

Why? _____

Why? _____

Why? _____

Why? _____

Why? _____

Why? _____

Why? _____

Why? _____

Why? _____

If you would like to explore this further, turn to page 208 in the Appendix and work with the exercise entitled "Identifying Your Beliefs."

HOW BELIEFS AFFECT YOUR LIFE

Preprogrammed agendas in our subconscious minds form the basis of what we choose to create and call "reality" in our lives. Thus, long-held beliefs can sabotage your life. You can accomplish only what you deeply believe is possible and what matches your internal picture about the world. Therefore, to create a more positive outcome and achieve what you consciously choose, you must let go of negative beliefs.

> You can accomplish only what you deeply believe is possible and what matches your internal picture about the world.

Pay attention to the patterns in your life. Do you have constant "dramas" going on? Do you feel like no matter what you do, it never works out? If you believe that you create your own reality, then you understand that you control—and are responsible for—your life. With this knowledge, you really can't fail.

You already know how you create fear when you feel like you have lost control. When your beliefs are driven by your fears rather than your hopes and dreams, you become stuck and draw negative experiences into your life. For example, if you believe that nobody likes you, then you will experience having no friends. If you believe that you never get what you want, your experiences will focus on always pleasing others.

Until you see the connection between your beliefs and your experiences, you will remain a victim. Once you understand this, however, you can choose to uncover the negative beliefs that don't serve you any more and change them to positive beliefs. Instead of saying, "My life is a mess," you can say, "I am changing my life."

> For every experience that is repeated, we have a belief that causes us to continue to create the experience.

Because your beliefs have such a profound effect on your life, it is vital that your beliefs support what you *really* want. There is a saying, "Be careful what you ask for, because you may get it!"

You may be unaware that one of your core beliefs is causing you to experience the opposite of what you think you want. The next case study illustrates this.

■ Case Study #26: The Promotion & The Baseball Game

A man we'll call Kenneth came to me for help one day. He felt very stressed over a possible job promotion, and he was worried that another guy was going to get the job. When I asked Kenneth why he thought that, he said, "Because it just seems like the other guy always gets it instead of me."

I then asked him, "Can you recall a time when you were younger and you asked for someone else to get something instead of you?" Kenneth's eyes became very large and he recalled being 12 years old on the baseball field. A fly ball was coming at him, the game was tied, and he didn't want to drop the ball. He remembered praying, "Dear God, give it to the other guy. I don't want to drop it." He believed that another boy would do a better job, since he wasn't good enough. A second opportunity to put himself in front occurred when Kenneth was up to bat later in the game. Once again, the game was tied. Instead of swinging the bat, he froze. He was afraid he would lose the game by striking out.

We worked through this fear and helped Kenneth to change his subconscious belief. By having him return in his mind to that baseball game and experience the feeling of catching the ball, he was able to change his belief to, "I am good enough to catch the ball." Then it was fairly easy for him to believe, "I am good enough for this job." He practiced seeing his name on the door and how it would feel to work in the new office. Instead of putting all of his eggs in another guy's basket, he kept them in his own. And he got the new job!

Sometimes, negative beliefs can contribute to painful, even dangerous, consequences. Look at the next case study.

■ *Case Study #27: Abuse On The Bus*

I once worked with a 13-year-old boy who was getting beaten up on the bus. When I asked him why he thought he was always picked on by his classmates, he replied, "Because, wherever I go everyone beats on me. Maybe God thinks I deserve it." He then told me about the amount of physical abuse that had been inflicted on him ever since his stepfather moved in nine years earlier.

After this young teenager understood how his belief that he deserved to be beaten could contribute to the physical experience itself, he worked on changing that belief. When he knew that he was enough—i.e., a valuable person worthy of respect—he didn't have to be beaten or punished anymore. Before too long, the abuse on the bus stopped. He no longer attracted into his life the type of kids that like to beat on other people.

BELIEFS & LOW SELF-ESTEEM

Many people share with me how their spouses or partners abuse them. They are caught up in the belief that beatings express how much a person loves you. This is reinforced when abusers use justifications, such as the ones below, to place responsibility for the problem on the abused child or partner.

- ■ "I only beat you because I love you."
- ■ "It makes me so unhappy when you misbehave."
- ■ "Why do you force me to beat you?"
- ■ "I only do it because I care about you. You need to learn what is right and what is wrong."

Many people believe that they deserved the beatings they received when they were children. One man shared with me how he grew up believing that all families beat their children after visitors leave.

Chapter 5 describes how fear affects people when their self-esteem is low and how the reactive brain's responses can lead them into abusive situations. By understanding how low self-esteem can trigger an abusive physical or emotional reaction, people can begin to accept—and sometimes even forgive—the parent, boyfriend, spouse, or adult who abused them. This can be a long and difficult healing process. Yet, in order to be healthy and free of the past, it is important for individuals who have experienced abuse to let go of their anger and choose to forgive. Without forgiveness, they remain stuck and connected to the abuser.

We learned earlier that anger is caused when we believe that someone or something doesn't see us as worthy—as good enough. Adults and children both struggle with low self-esteem. Even though adults may have grown up and become parents, they still carry wounded little boys and little girls inside. Adults/parents are just people doing the best they can with what they know. Inside every abusive adult is a scared little boy or girl who doesn't know any other way to keep under control their fear of not being enough. They believe they need to fight or control others in order to survive. They have yet to discover their self-worth.

Remember, the only reason we put another person down is to pull ourselves up. The lower our self-esteem, the more we slash away at others. **When we believe in ourselves, we don't need to hurt other people or buy into their fears.** By understanding and accepting our feelings and who we are, we can choose to not let our reactive brain control us.

RELATIONSHIPS & BELIEFS

Our relationships are also based upon our beliefs. When a person believes that he/she can't trust people who say, "I love you" because they always leave, that person will continually attract partners who aren't trustworthy and who do leave.

■ *Case Study #28: Jenny's Needy Men*

Jenny told me that she was sick and tired of attracting losers in her life. She was living with a man who she felt was taking her for granted and using her. When asked why she continued to stay with him, Jenny replied, "At least I have someone. He'll change and things will get better."

Jenny's belief was, "I need to be needed to be loved." She drew needy men into her life because she didn't believe that a healthy man, who had his life under control, would love her.

Too often, we stay in bad relationships because we are afraid of being alone. We will even try to change our partners into what we think we want them to be, settling for less than what we really want.

> ...we always have exactly what we believe we want or need.

The truth is, we always have exactly what we believe we want or need. When we are afraid of losing someone because we're afraid of being alone, what we *believe* is, "I can't survive without someone to take care of me."

On the other hand, when our self-esteem is sound, we don't *need* to have someone; we *choose* to share life with someone. When we love ourselves and want to have loving relationships, we draw people who love us into our lives.

Our relationships are mirrors for the truth of what we believe about ourselves. If you see a pattern in your relationships with which you are unhappy, look in your mirror. See why you keep repeating the pattern. Have you spent most of your life living out a childhood belief? Perhaps now is the time to change the belief and thus change the pattern.

■ Case Study #29: Plastic Partners

When I was dating after my divorce, I saw a pattern of what I called plastic partners in my life. They were nice men; they just didn't seem to be able to get below the surface emotionally. They didn't have the depth I thought I was looking for.

When I finally explored why I was bringing this type of person into my life, I discovered that I was afraid of becoming emotionally attached to someone again after going through a painful divorce. I didn't trust that love could last. When I got out of the Whiner mode and regained my self-esteem, a wonderful loving man entered my life.

Many teenagers and adults go through tremendously painful experiences as they try to find the right person to love. They may have a clear history of repeatedly attracting the same type of person, and yet be totally blind about how these relationships reflect their beliefs.

For example, a woman who was fed up with men made the following statement in one of my classes: "It doesn't matter where I am. I draw any man who lies and cheats on women to me." When she discovered the core belief behind her words, she realized that she believed all men lie and cheat because her father had an affair.

A young man in another class was convinced that the only thing women wanted from him was his wallet. He believed that he wasn't good enough by himself; he had to be needed or pay to get people to love him. This man attracted many women who needed financial saviors. Their needs fed his belief, and vice versa.

Once individuals understand how their relationships mirror their beliefs about themselves, they can change their view of themselves as victims and draw in healthy relationships. Thus, even in relationship issues, we really do have what we believe we want.

BLAMING OTHERS

Often, we are blind to why we draw certain experiences and people to us. We choose to blame others for our problems, labeling them as not being good enough in some way. Yet, just because we feel that a person isn't right for us doesn't mean that person needs to change to be enough. **A particular person may not be good for us, but that person is still good enough in his/her own right.**

Perhaps a person was perfect for us at a certain time because he/she filled a need that we have now outgrown. This is true in all relationships: friendships, marriages, work partners, etc. Let's look at marriages for example. Some couples work on growing together and nurturing each other's individual growth. Over time, this creates a new and healthier relationship for them. Some couples choose to separate when one or both of the individuals outgrow the original dynamics of the relationship. In either case, the people involved are choosing to discover and learn in their own way about who they are and what they believe they need.

When we fall into the pattern of blaming someone else for letting us down in a relationship, we remain stuck in a victim mind frame—forgetting that we created the opportunity to let go of someone or something in order to move on and continue to grow. The more we understand and love ourselves, the more we can lose this victim complex and accept responsibility for creating our lives around our beliefs. Let's look at a couple of specific ways this plays out in our lives.

Have you ever been fired? Instead of coming from a victim point of view and blaming your boss for firing you, explore how you helped to create that experience. Perhaps deep down inside you wanted to move on to another opportunity, but were afraid to take the necessary actions. Or perhaps you blame a teacher for flunking you in a course. Did you choose to not turn in your work because you believed you would fail anyway?

Blame creates a heavy load of negative baggage to lug around through life. Remember, it's not about the other guy—it's always about you. If a little voice inside says, **"Why me?"** say back to yourself, **"Why not you?"** Then leave the baggage of blame behind. Getting back at a former partner, a teacher, or a boss may feel good temporarily, but in the long run it only hurts you. If you continue to play the victim, you will be stuck wallowing in and repeating the past. And when you carry too much baggage from the past, you aren't free to embrace your future. By owning your choices in life, you allow yourself the freedom and space to move on to the next opportunity.

CHANGE & LETTING GO

We miss many opportunities that come into our lives because we focus on negative beliefs and fears. These two things can keep us in jobs and relationships that we have outgrown. Do any of these sound familiar?

- I can't leave you and take this job.
- I'm afraid that I will be alone all my life if I break up with my girlfriend.
- This may be bad, but at least I can count on it.

The fear of letting go is directly related to the belief that we will not survive if we change. When we attach ourselves intensely to someone or something, we feel like we lose a part of ourselves when we are separated from that person or thing. We've all heard the saying, "Nothing lasts forever," but we like to believe that it will.

In order for us to grow, we must let go of our fear of loss and create the space for new opportunities to come into our lives. It isn't possible to fill a cup with root beer when it's already full of milk. You first have to dump out the milk. **Whenever you create space, life will find a way to fill it up.** Sometimes, you cannot really know who you are until you let go of what you've been holding onto. Only by letting go will you be able to embrace all that you are and can be.

Many people are afraid of being alone. Yet we all need to be alone at times—to discover who we really are without being under the immediate influence of others. When we learn to enjoy ourselves and see that we can survive on our own, we become stronger and healthier.

Almost every day I hear someone share with me how unhappy they are being alone. From their perspective, they are the loneliest people in the world. They are the only ones without someone. "Everybody except me has someone. What's wrong with me?"

Isn't it strange that what we focus on seems to multiply out in the world? Have you ever noticed that when you break a leg, a lot more people seem to be using crutches? If you buy a red car, you are convinced that suddenly a lot more people are driving red cars. And when you focus on being alone, you see couples everywhere.

Letting go is one of the most powerful processes we experience throughout our lives. It can be very difficult to let someone or something go when we believe that person or thing is vital to our survival. But the process we go through when we let go can be one of the greatest times of transformation in our lives. Whether we let go by choice or not, we are forced to trust that we will survive when we no longer have what we thought we needed. By

The more we advance through life, the more we have to let go. But the more we learn to let go, the more we gain.

seeing that we can survive loss and lack of control in life, we become stronger.

This process appears in all guises, both profound and mundane. Letting go can come through the loss of a relationship or a job, the death of a pet or a loved one, or just by changing our morning routine. **The more we advance through life, the more we have to let go. But the more we learn to let go, the more we gain.**

I have had personal experience with the difficult connection between beliefs and letting go. It took me a long time to learn to let go and be patient; I wanted things to happen *now*! I would quickly get upset with slow-moving cars, red lights, and waiting in line—in fact, anything that stopped me from continuing my life at its usual fast pace. My children even complained that I walked too fast when they shopped with me. I finally realized that the reason I was always in a hurry stemmed from two beliefs: that I would either be left out or I would let someone down. Both of these beliefs were based on childhood fears that I would be left out, forgotten, or not loved if I let someone down. Now, whenever my impatience rears its ugly head, I remind myself, "Take time to smell the roses. Everyone will be fine, life will go on, and everything is in order." My motto for my life is, "If it doesn't flow, let it go."

"If it doesn't flow, let it go."

SURVIVAL TECHNIQUES & BELIEFS

When we believe that we are not good enough or able to cope, we create all types of survival techniques. We will even give ourselves up to control our world and be safe. In chapter 5, we covered four techniques that we use to control our world (Bully, Accuser, Shielder, and Whiner). One very common technique that is connected to the Whiner is what I call the "Good Girl/Good Boy" or "Chameleon." These people have the following beliefs:

- If I do what you want me to do and be what you want me to be, I will be loved.
- I need to please you to be loved.
- If I give myself up, I am lovable and I will survive.

Ultimately, Good Girls/Good Boys will change themselves in whatever way they feel is necessary in order to be loved and accepted. To change these beliefs, Good Girls/ Good Boys need to change their viewpoint. They need to learn that they are fine just as they are; they don't have to meet others' expectations in order to be loved.

Many bright students are put on a pedestal. Comments like, "Oh, we never have to worry about Jill," or "We don't have a worry in the world about Mark; he never lets us down," should send out an alarm. Jill or Mark might be giving up themselves in order to be what other people want them to be. Many high achievers, or "perfect" sons and daughters, end up rebelling later. Some will unknowingly decide to cover up a family dysfunction and become the "good kid," while another sibling may become the "black sheep," calling attention to the dysfunction.

The following brief essay was written by a beautiful, talented high school girl who was struggling with the Chameleon complex. She agreed to let me include it in this book in order to help other teens who feel the same way.

I'm so lost. If people would only take the time to look into my eyes and see that I have something to say, if only they would take the time to listen. But that is not the way my world works. All that everyone is allowed to be is a shell. A shell that, the longer it is kept, the less and less the person inside becomes. People prance around never seeing anyone for more than what is only skin deep. So much that the connection is so thin that it can break in only an instant. And then that whole world crumbles, and falls. Sure, in a few moments everything will be rebuilt to the normal state of things, but how hard is it to rebuild the first few steps of a never-ending staircase? It crumbles, falls, then is restored over and over. Never going above those first steps, never getting ahead, only circling around that same stage of emptiness.

A relationship can only be successful if built from the inside out. A person cannot be made pure from outer perfection. But pureness will never fail to bring true and endless love and beauty from all angles. So, please, someone find me. Look into my eyes and see that I have something to say. Be that one to listen. Change my world, break my shell, help me find myself.

— Beth, age 16

Becoming someone we aren't in order to survive creates a lot of stifled anger and confusion. It is often the Chameleons who carry a volcano inside, ready to explode. Some say they feel like they have two people inside themselves: one who is good and one who is bad. Others eventually become numb to their real feelings.

When we give up who we really are, we push our spirit deep within until we feel as though we'll burst. That is when the anger and pain involved with giving ourselves up begins to surface. At this point, some individuals turn to drugs or run away in an attempt to rediscover themselves. Giving ourselves up to please someone else can be a very painful experience when we finally realize that we do not feel emotionally connected to who we really are.

We dance many dances around and for each other in order to be loved. In any dysfunctional situation, there is a control dance in which everyone involved is stepping to the beat. This dance can occur in a partnership, a friendship, a family, an organization, a company, or a classroom. When you see any of the control techniques that were discussed in chapter 5, look for the beliefs that are feeding the fear. How is that fear being acted out? Through bullying or, perhaps, accusing? Who believes that their needs aren't being met? Who feels that they have lost the control they need in order to feel safe?

DISCONNECTING FROM POWER TAKERS

Stop for a moment, get a piece of paper, and make a list of the top four people or things that you feel are draining your energy. (Remember the image of the power tank strapped to your back from chapter 5?) What do you fear the most? Who do you worry about? Who are you angry with? These are your major power takers.

Now, imagine that you have tubes connected to your power tank from each of these four power takers. If the total capacity of your tank is 10 units, evaluate how much power/energy you are giving away to each of the power takers. Use a scale of 1–10, and write an amount next to each item. This is not an exact measurement, and there is no "right" answer. Just indicate what feels accurate to you. Here is an example.

POWER TAKER	AMOUNT OF POWER/ENERGY GIVEN
Money	6 units
Parents	3 units
Job	5 units
Health	3 units
Total	**17 units**

If your power tank holds 10 units of energy, how much are you over your limit? With a total of 17 units, this individual feels she is at least seven units over the limit.

Now, what are your dreams for the future? Choose one. For example, you might want to buy a new car. How much power/energy from your power tank do you need to create your dream? Let's say that you feel you need five units of energy.

You need five units of energy for your future and you are already seven units beyond your tank's capacity just in supporting your power takers. Your tank is empty; in fact, you're overdrawn. Where will you get the extra energy to supply your power takers and still create your dreams? YOUR BODY!

When your tank is empty, you will push your body to keep going. Can you see the picture? Imagine that your car has run out of gas and you are physically pushing it down the road. It won't be long until you are so worn out that you collapse.

Unless you choose to disconnect from your major power takers, you will run down your body and not have enough energy to create your future. Then, you are not only stuck, tired, depressed, and angry because you've lost your power, you are also a prime target for disease or an accident.

So what can you do about this? ***Change the picture!!***

By disconnecting from your power takers, you will have more energy in your tank. Let's use the four power takers from the example on the previous page to see how to do this.

MONEY

What are you concerned about? Ask yourself, "What's the worst that could happen?" Yes, you could go bankrupt. Could you survive that? Would you still be okay? When you focus on not having enough money, this keeps "not having enough money" as part of your life. Disconnect from that fear—right now. Give yourself back six units of power.

PARENTS

What are you dealing with? Are there any control issues? Can you see why you are giving your power away? What do you gain by doing this? What is your fear based on? Change your belief, let go of the fear, and give yourself back three units of power.

JOB

Do you hate your job? Why? Have you started looking for another one, or are you taking steps to open your own business? In the meantime, see your current job as a stepping stone that is preparing you for your future. Say to yourself, "I am creating the perfect place for me to work." When you do this, give yourself back five units of energy.

HEALTH

Give your body positive thoughts every day. Say to yourself, "I am healthy and strong, and I choose to remain healthy." You have already gained back 14 units of energy, so you know that your health will be better with less stress in your life. Give yourself three units of power.

When you have disconnected from all of your power takers, you can replenish your tank and direct a full 10 units of your energy toward taking care of yourself and your future. You are no longer giving your energy away.

When your body is on empty, you feel weak and depressed. Depression can be biochemically and/or emotionally based. However, since the body and mind work together, fear plays a very important part in both of these causes for depression.

Depression feeds fear. So instead of saying, "I'm depressed," and dwelling on that, ask yourself, "Why am I depressed?" Then identify the fear behind your depression. Once you understand the fear, you may discover the beliefs that are influencing your body and emotions. This isn't easy to do, since we are often in deep denial about our fear. Yet identifying and facing your fear may help you change your beliefs and, perhaps, ultimately move you out of depression. The next case study illustrates this.

■ *Case Study #30: Depressed About Dollars*

Roxanne was depressed about her money situation; she was afraid she wouldn't have enough to pay her bills. She had grown up in a family with 12 children. Although she was now out on her own and had a good job, she still believed, "There is not enough for me to survive."

Once Roxanne understood how focusing on not having enough led her to create what she believed, she realized that she had to change her belief and let go of the fear. She decided that bankruptcy was the worst situation that could happen to her, and she agreed that she could always survive bankruptcy. Once she knew that she could always survive, Roxanne was able to take back control from the fear that was draining her and let go of the depression.

You have to disconnect from power takers in order to maintain good health and create your future. When you stay connected to your past or wrapped up in your fears, you become stuck—spinning your wheels or sitting still with an empty energy tank.

REBUILDING & PLANTING

What happens after you let go, after you empty the tank? This can be one of the scariest times in life. A feeling of loss or emptiness comes forth, creating the sense that you actually did lose a part of yourself in the process. Your former life and connections with people, roles, and activities must be filled with new people, roles, and activities.

This process occurs whenever there is a significant disruption in your life—e.g., when you leave a relationship or lose friends, when you are laid off or fired from your job, or when a family member dies. At these times of transition, familiar past connections with others and former ways of being in the world are broken. We experience a void in time, space, people, and feelings. The feelings of being disconnected and lost can be very painful.

After surviving the feelings of loss, we may realize that this change will result in a greater understanding of who we really are. It is a time to reconstruct and begin again. It is a magical and exciting time that might be disguised as a lonely and scary void. Yet, time heals. And voids in life are always filled with new experiences. As hard as it may be, you only need to let go and allow life to fill the space—it always does.

I have experienced the process of letting go and rebuilding through divorce, as well as the loss of my parents and other close relationships. My divorce helped me to grow and see the truth about myself. Although it was one of the most painful experiences I've ever gone through, it was also the one that forced me to stretch and expand beyond what I would have ever thought possible. I began to see life much more clearly. I now realize that it takes two to divorce, and that all relationships serve as mirrors which reflect our inner beliefs.

What we want from others, we have to give to ourselves first. To be loved completely for who we are, we must love ourselves just as we are. To be treated with respect, we must first respect ourselves. Too often we put our needs onto others and expect them to fulfill those needs. Then we're hurt when we don't get what we want!

> **What we want from others, we have to give to ourselves first.**

I always wanted flowers. I felt disappointed when they weren't delivered to my door on my birthday or for no special reason. I couldn't understand why other women had men who treated them to flowers while I didn't. The poem, *After A While*, helped me realize that I needed to plant my own garden rather than waiting for

someone to send me flowers. When I finally planted
seeds to nurture myself, my life began to blossom. In fact,
I even began to receive flowers at my doorstep!

After A While
by Veronica A. Shoffstall

After a while, you learn the subtle difference
between holding a hand and chaining a soul,

And you learn that love doesn't mean leaning
And company doesn't mean security,

And you begin to learn that kisses aren't contracts
And presents aren't promises,

And you begin to accept your defeats
With your head up and your eyes open
With the grace of a woman, not the grief of a child,

And you learn to build all your roads on today
because tomorrow's ground is too uncertain for plans,
And futures have a way of falling down in mid-flight.

After a while, you learn that even the sunshine burns
if you get too much.

So you plant your own garden and decorate your own soul,
instead of waiting for someone to bring you flowers.

And you learn that you really can endure…
that you really are strong.
And you really do have worth.
And you learn and learn…
with every goodbye you learn.

After you let go, you need to find some soil and seeds
for a flower garden. You also need to take action—to start
planting new nurturing seeds for self-growth and become
the gardener of your life.

The ability to change your life is just a thought away
if you change your beliefs. For example, if you believe
there is no such thing as failure, then you can't fail.
Instead, you'll see what others may call "failure" as an
opportunity to choose a path that is different from the
one you're on.

BELIEFS ABOUT JUDGMENT & FAILURE

What if we looked at most of our experiences in life as just growth processes instead of judging them as good or bad experiences? Of course, that would eliminate our testing, evaluation, and judgment systems for everything we do in life!

Many times we ask questions like, "Was it right of her to do that?" "Don't you think that's wrong?" "Do you think he will be good for me?" We judge everything and everyone based on our beliefs and filtered through a perspective of love or fear. But what if life is just a process full of experiences that includes ups and downs?

If we look at life through the eyes of a toddler, perhaps we can see what failure is and what it isn't. We were all once babies learning to walk. While we did this, we experienced many falls and spent a lot of time picking ourselves up and starting over. If we had believed that we had "failed" each time we fell, we probably would never have learned to walk. The desire to walk was so strong that falling became just part of the process of getting to the goal. It wasn't a big deal. In fact, each time our legs had to push us back up, they became stronger and sturdier.

There is another example of this "no-failure" process in the natural world. If you help a butterfly break free of its cocoon, it will fall to its death when it emerges and tries to fly. Its wings are just too weak to carry its weight. To survive, a butterfly must go through the process of struggling to break free from its cocoon. Without this struggle, it cannot strengthen its wings. Without strong wings, the butterfly cannot fly. And we certainly don't call the butterfly a failure as it attempts to free itself from its cocoon!

It seems to be human nature to make judgments and label things in life as good or bad. However, we are often too blinded by our fears to see the whole picture.

How many times have you judged something as bad, then later looked back and realized that it was one of the best things that could have happened to you? We may

It seems to be human nature to make judgments and label things in life as good or bad. make the judgment that a person arrested for shoplifting is in a bad situation. Yet, for that person to find his/her truth and heal, perhaps that's what needed to happen. From this perspective, the shoplifting arrest would be considered positive. So even though you may not understand why something is happening to you, let go of your judgments and choose to see each experience as a learning opportunity.

Of course, there are times when we must make judgments. Without established rules of conduct, we would have no way to respond when an individual deliberately chooses to hurt someone else. Although society has developed specific rules within a structured form of government to protect individual rights, we still have the opportunity to represent our beliefs on how such actions should be judged and dealt with.

As for our own actions, we constantly serve as our own judge and jury. **When we're able to let go of the judge inside, we can understand that people don't fail; they are just under construction.**

It may be helpful to see life from the perspective that William Shakespeare defined for us—a stage on which we all are actors performing many parts. It is possible to observe our performance on the stage of life without making judgments that we are "good" or "bad." When we get tangled up in these judgments, we need to find the belief that our fear is based upon. Then, we can take our understanding of the mind and heart connection and apply what we know to what we experience. This will help us to see the whole picture in a situation, let go of our judgments, and reframe the experience.

In the last six chapters we have explored how our thoughts, actions, and beliefs each play a role in why we do what we do. There is one more vital piece to understanding the whole picture—the body. Our thoughts and beliefs also affect our body's health and actions. The next chapter explains the body's wisdom—how it listens to our thoughts and communicates to us.

CHAPTER 7
YOUR BODY'S WISDOM

■ ■ ■

*"I don't eat junk food and
I don't think junk thoughts."*

～ Pilgrim Lady ～
SPEAKER, AUTHOR & WALKER FOR PEACE

Your body has great wisdom. It hears everything you say out loud or to yourself. In fact, your body responds to absolutely everything. If you would like to see this in action, turn to the exercise called "Check Your Body's Wisdom" on page 209 in the Appendix.

In chapter 6 we saw how beliefs affect what we do and feel. Beliefs, and their accompanying thoughts, also influence our bodies—even to the point of generating illness or helping us heal ourselves.

Your body mirrors your emotions and thoughts.

Your body mirrors your emotions and thoughts. Because you have a body, you are able to physically act on your thoughts and intentions. Your body protects and warns you. Your body carries you through life, responding to whatever your mind tells it. Just like your brain, if you don't use it, you can lose it. If you neglect your body by feeding it the wrong foods or not getting enough rest and exercise, it will become run down.

You know already that your beliefs and feelings affect your mind and body, which continually work together. This includes your subconscious mind (Level 2), which can influence and even over-ride both your conscious mind (Level 1) and your body.

THE SUBCONSCIOUS MIND

To understand how thoughts affect your body, it is necessary to know how the subconscious mind works.

The subconscious mind is subjective. It doesn't judge things as right or wrong; it just accepts what you tell it. Therefore, when you say repeatedly that you are tired, your body accepts this as literally true. You will be tired.

Have you ever experienced a time when you felt just fine, but people told you how tired and pale you looked? Maybe they even asked you if you felt sick. If enough people made these comments, did you begin to feel a little weak and sick?

Children who are afraid of school can make them-selves sick by just thinking about going to school when they get up in the morning. Adults can get sick on the morning of a job interview. They are not "faking it," by the way. They *are* physically ill, but the cause is an underlying belief, fear, or thought, not exposure to a germ.

What we tell ourselves most often, our subconscious mind will believe. That is why it is so important for us to pay attention to our thoughts and to focus on positive results or actions.

> **What we tell ourselves most often, our subconscious mind will believe.**

Focusing on the positive takes work; it doesn't happen automatically. As soon as a negative thought appears, you need to erase it by telling yourself several positive statements.

For example, do you think that you are going to get sick every time you have to give a speech? If so, your body will help you to feel sick. Are you concerned that you will trip when you're running in a race? If you spend time worrying about it, the chances are very good that you will fall.

The beauty of the body/mind connection is that this programming can also work the other way. If you believe that you are smart and will do well on a test that you've prepared for, you probably will do well. You can also win a race that you have prepared your mind and body to win.

■ *Case Study #31: Sick About Tests*

Susan usually became sick whenever she took a big test. She worried ahead of time that she would get sick, and was especially concerned that she couldn't leave the testing room if she did become ill. She was all but convinced that she could never pass her upcoming pharmaceutical exam.

After years of experiencing her fear of getting sick during tests, Susan's body believed that tests made her sick. So we reprogrammed her subconscious mind from the negative statement, "I always get sick when I take a test," to the positive statement, "I am healthy, relaxed, and the answers come easily to me when I take a test." Later, Susan told me that she had eaten a large breakfast before the exam and never felt sick. And the best part? She passed the test!

One of the most common reasons people do not do well on tests is their fear of failure. They may have developed this fear at a very young age, and now the fear continues into their adult lives. How can that happen? First, you experience what it feels like to fail a test. The more painful the experience, the more deeply it is embedded in your body and mind. Your body reacts, and you go into fear mode—perhaps causing physical symptoms such as a racing heart or an upset stomach. You start thinking negatively—perhaps telling yourself that this feels terrible, that you're a stupid person, and that you'll probably fail again. Then you begin to believe you can't control the outcome. At this point, a vicious cycle has been established; you are preparing to flunk once again. If you do fail another test, the body reaction/ negative thinking/belief/failure pattern gets reinforced and continues.

"FEAR OF FAILURE" CYCLE

FAIL TEST

BODY REACTS "Fear mode"

NEGATIVE THINKING STARTS "I'll fail again"

BELIEF FORMED "I have no control"

How can this cycle be broken? By changing your negative belief, you can change the negative pattern of flunking tests. As you successfully take tests, you no longer believe that you will inevitably fail. Finally, your body begins to believe in a positive rather than a negative outcome.

USING THE SUBCONSCIOUS MIND

The subconscious mind can help the body heal, perform, and relax when under stressful situations. The United States Army trains soldiers to use their subconscious minds to help them through difficult situations when they are physically confined. A prisoner of war has described how he imagined running five miles a day to help keep his mind and body in shape while he was confined in a cell during the Vietnam War.

Think of your subconscious mind as your personal genie. Many people link the subconscious mind to divine intervention, angelic communication, or their own Higher Self. You can apply your own beliefs. The bottom line is whatever you tell or ask your subconscious mind to do, it

> ...whatever you tell your subconscious mind to do, it will work hard to achieve. It never rests.

will work hard to achieve. It never rests. Once you give your subconscious its "marching orders," it will do everything possible to fulfill them. Therefore, if you want to experience a positive, rewarding, loving life, you need to make sure your subconscious mind knows that!

Once you identify a goal to focus on (preferably something that is positive for you and/or others), your subconscious mind will constantly bring ideas and opportunities to you that are related to that goal. What you ask for may not happen right away—maybe not for a long time. But be assured, if you focus on it, your subconscious mind will continue to work hard to bring that vision to you.

Even when you sleep, your subconscious works for you. Have you ever awakened in the morning talking to yourself as though you were completing a conversation with yourself? You probably were speaking with your subconscious.

Your subconscious mind communicates by using symbols, images, gut feelings, and intuition; it isn't big on logical, linear processes. It will often flash a quick message to you or give you a strong urge to act on something. Many people have experienced a common form of this. You think about someone "out of the blue" whom you haven't seen or thought about in months. Then you suddenly meet them on the street, or they just happen to give you a call. As you learn how to more effectively listen to your subconscious mind, you will become aware of more positive opportunities to act upon.

If things don't appear to be going the way we wish, we may blame life for dumping on us. We forget that, even though we think we know what we want, we can sabotage the outcome. A woman told me that she really wanted to meet the right man for her instead of all the unavailable ones she'd been meeting. I said, "OK, Mr. Right is standing on the other side of this door. Go over and open it." She recoiled in her chair and said, "No, I'm not ready!" She was purposely meeting unavailable men because she was emotionally unavailable. Her subconscious mind was taking care of her, giving her what she *really* wanted.

■ *Case Study #32: The Injured Athlete*

Andy was a competitive athlete in field and track. He injured himself every time he was in a tournament. Andy said that he wanted to prove to everyone that he was the best at running the hurdles. Yet, every time he had the opportunity to prove it, Andy eliminated himself from the competition with an injury.

After processing why he created the injuries, he realized that he really didn't believe he could win. He didn't even like running the hurdles. Andy ran because he wanted his father to be proud of him. His belief that he wasn't good enough to win caused him to sabotage his performance with an injury. He created the injury to avoid failing and possibly losing his father's approval and love.

PROGRAMMING THE POSITIVE

You can begin to change negative beliefs—and your experiences in the world—by choosing to create positive thoughts. Change your negative thoughts into positive affirmations. Instead of saying, "My life is a mess," say, "I am constructing a new life." Instead of saying, "I hate my job," say, "I create a wonderful place to work." Write positive statements about what you want in life and place them around your house, in your car, and at work. If you say affirmations like the ones on the next page to yourself every day, you will program your subconscious mind to believe them.

- I am enough.
- I am healthy.
- I am able to freely give and receive love.
- I can create my life to be anything I choose it to be.
- I live every day with happiness and love.

When you say affirmations to yourself over and over again, your subconscious mind believes that they are *already* true. Therefore, it is especially powerful if you can see yourself as currently living your hopes and dreams—even if they aren't there quite yet. Meanwhile, cut out pictures and look at them every day. To program the positive, you need to imagine that what you wish for is on its way to you. In fact, you need to imagine that it has already arrived!

As mentioned in chapter 1, athletes have known about the power of positive thinking for many years. They know how important it is to believe that they are winners; they use their imagination to see themselves crossing the finish line, winning a medal, or hitting a home run.

If you can see it, you can be it!

Seeing something in your mind as if it has already happened is one of the most effective and powerful ways to program your mind and body for success. If you can see it, you can be it!

PROCESSING PATTERNS & PROGRAMMING

As we saw in chapter 3, people have different patterns for processing information, so some people have difficulty picturing outcomes in their minds (e.g., KAVs or AKVs). These individuals need to *feel* what something would be like before their minds can see a picture of it.

Case Study #33: The Invisible Basketball

Once, when I was a classroom teacher, I asked my students to picture a basketball. A girl raised her hand and said that she couldn't picture a basketball in her mind. I had her stand up, and I pretended to throw a basketball to her. She caught the pretend ball.

Then I asked her, "Why did you catch the ball if you couldn't see it?" She looked perplexed and said, "Because you threw it to me." She couldn't see it until she experienced what it felt like to catch it.

I also learned this lesson from a woman whom I was helping with pain control. When I asked her to *see* (i.e., visualize) the pain in her back as a ball, she shook her head and told me she couldn't do that. Then I asked her to *feel* the pain in the same way. She didn't have any problem feeling the pain as a ball.

People who can't picture things clearly in their minds are usually Level 3, visually unconscious processors. They find it difficult to process visual information. It is important for teachers, trainers, and coaches to remember this when they want to teach someone an abstract concept. The people receiving the information may not be able to visually understand something unless they have the opportunity to experience it first through their bodies.

PROGRAMMING THE SUBCONSCIOUS FOR HEALING

When you use your Level 1 (conscious) sense—whether it is visual, auditory, or kinesthetic—to program your subconscious, amazing things can happen.

When you use your Level 1 (conscious) sense—whether it is visual, auditory, or kinesthetic—to program your subconscious, amazing things can happen. For example, every day, people are using their subconscious minds to heal their bodies. Hospitals are teaching children how to use their imagination to fight cancer cells. Patients are shrinking tumors and healing incisions by pretending that they're painting soothing white light on the wounds. These are just two examples of programming strategies that have emerged from a relatively new area of medicine called psychoneuroimmunology.

Since the mind and body can work together to help the body heal, imaging, biofeedback, visualization, and hypnotherapy are very useful tools for patients in any medical situation. I have met individuals who had operations without any anesthesia and successfully used their imagination to overcome pain. Doctors are finding it helpful when their patients use their subconscious minds for healing. Patients who undergo hypnotherapy before an operation usually bleed less and heal faster than those who do not.

SOUND & COLOR

My good friend and mentor, Dr. David Frederick, teaches individuals how to work with the built-in healing systems of their bodies. Using music, sound, and energy, he inspires his students to take control of their own healing process and program their minds for wellness. Dr. Frederick also teaches health care practitioners how to help individuals heal themselves by using noninvasive techniques. (More information about Dr. Frederick is included in the Appendix on page 225.)

For example, although there is controversy about how effective classical music is in helping people to learn, our experience has shown that some students can increase their ability to concentrate and recall information when they listen to Mozart or Bach as they study. Some corporations use classical music in certain work areas to help their employees maintain their focus. And now, there is mounting evidence that this musically-enhanced ability to concentrate can also be used to support healing.

Music and color are both based on vibrational frequencies, and both are proving to be effective tools for healing and learning. For each of us, color and music play a major role in how we feel. This is because they trigger reactions in us at all three levels—unconscious, subconscious, and conscious.

Have you ever noticed how your mood changes when you listen to different types of music? Just playing a favorite song from your past can take you back to how you felt when you were younger. And what about your favorite outfit? What colors do you enjoy wearing? You can use color and music to help program your mind for healing, financial success, or anything else you desire.

PAIN

Although it is not pleasant, pain is also part of our body's wisdom. Pain of any kind promotes change. It is our

Pain of any kind promotes change.

body's way of telling us that we need to pay attention to some kind of imbalance. Pain must not be ignored; it is a warning message that we send directly to ourselves.

We've all experienced how pain can influence our behavior physically. When we sprain an ankle, we usually don't put our full weight on that leg until it begins to heal; we limp. But not all pain is quite so obvious. We may be "limping" from previous emotional pain— unwittingly reinforcing negative beliefs and programming ourselves for even more pain.

For example, when we are angry or afraid, we often squelch our feelings and store our emotions in our body. When we have too much anger or fear stored up physically, this can lead to pain or illness. It is important that we let go of negative feelings and not "stuff" them physically. Why?

It actually takes a lot of energy to stay angry or afraid. We need this energy to heal ourselves and to focus on a healthy future instead of our past. We cannot reprogram our beliefs effectively when a lot of our energy is being used up in coping with pain, anger, and fear. By letting go of anger and fear, we may discover that we've let go of pain as well. Then, with a healthier body, we have more energy to program our subconscious in the directions we wish and to pursue our passions in life!

HUMOR

Humor is one of the best tools we have in our body's "tool box" for healing. Humor is a wonderful and natural healing remedy. It's a supply of self-medication built

> "Good health is a laughing matter— and that's nothing to sneeze at!"
>
> — Patch Adams, M.D.

within each of us. Best of all, it's free and you don't need a prescription to use it!

Humor can heal all kinds of pain. Many patients with life-threatening illnesses are deliberately including humor in their lives to promote their own healing. Medical research has shown that when we laugh, biochemical changes occur that promote the healing process.

In addition, when we can laugh—either at ourselves or with others—we stop taking life so seriously. Having the ability to see the humor in our lives allows us to step back and view things from a wider perspective.

I have had the opportunity to share some time with a wonderful doctor named Patch Adams, who lives and promotes "passionate humor" every day. Patch is currently creating his vision, which he describes as:

> "A medical project to address all the problems of one delivery system… by fully integrating all healing arts, living with patients (hospital is the staff's home), giving patients three- to four-hour initial interviews, being the first silly hospital, and integrating medicine with arts and crafts, performing arts, nature, agriculture, recreation, and social service."

Patch teaches those who are in the medical profession how to get closer to their patients with humor:

> "…one of the most important tenets of our philosophy is that health is based on happiness—from hugging and clowning around to finding joy in family and friends, satisfaction in work, and ecstasy in nature and the arts." [6]

He also reminds us that laughter is a powerful healing tool for the mind, body, and heart. Humor helps us to reach out from behind our barriers and connect with each other. It *is* soul medicine! (More information about Adams and his projects is included in the Appendix on page 224.)

Humor not only mends our bodies and hearts, but it can bridge gaps where human connections have been blocked by fear. When all else fails, appropriate humor can help people reach out to one another.

WHAT'S NEXT?

In this chapter we've explored several ways in which our body communicates with us, and how our body and subconscious mind are connected and influenced by our thoughts and beliefs. With the information from the previous chapters, you now have the necessary pieces to create a whole picture. In the next chapter you will learn how to apply this knowledge and practice viewing life's experiences from perspectives that can lead to positive changes for yourself and others.

IN THE MEANTIME

Would you like to experiment with some ways to relieve stress and sleep better? Turn to pages 211–214 in the Appendix at the back of this book, where you'll find two "sure-fire" relaxation techniques.

CHAPTER 8
REFRAMING THE PICTURE

■ ■ ■

"Everything that irritates us
about each other
can lead us to
an understanding
of ourselves."

～ Carl Jung ～
PSYCHOANALYST & AUTHOR

This chapter is about reframing the picture, i.e., reviewing how we look at things. To begin, I need to give you my definition of "reframing," since you're not likely to find it in a dictionary.

Reframing: The process of consciously changing perspectives. Seeing and understanding something from one perspective and then mentally shifting to a different perspective.

An example of reframing can be found in mystery stories in the familiar phrase, "He was framed." This means, of course, that someone has arranged pieces of evidence to make it appear as though another person is guilty of a crime. For the detective to solve the case and catch the guilty party, he has to assemble and examine all the pieces of evidence with no preconceived ideas. The detective must be able to mentally step back and reframe what he sees—looking at the evidence as though the person might be innocent rather than guilty.

As in a good mystery, when we are able to reframe how we view a particular situation, we can see past illusions and get to the truth. But too often, we focus on only one part of the picture, allowing our fears and prejudices to blind us.

You've probably heard the story about the three blind men who were asked to describe an elephant. One man felt its trunk and stated that the elephant was long and round, like a snake. The second man felt the elephant's ear, and he insisted that it was flat and soft, not like a snake at all. The third man thought the others were completely wrong. He felt the elephant's side and experienced something large and endless, like a mountain. They each thought they knew what an entire elephant looked like. They were all wrong, but from their individual, limited perspective they didn't know that. Only those who could step back and see the entire elephant at one time would understand that.

So it is when we are examining why we do what we do. In order to understand each other and ourselves, we need to consider how all the parts affect the whole. Focusing on only one part can cause us to lose sight of the truth—or be blind to it altogether. As we begin to understand why we think, feel, believe, and act the way we do, we can reframe our judgmental perspectives. We can see more clearly the whole elephant, the truth being shown to us.

Is reframing easy? No, it's not. Seeing a larger picture—a larger truth, if you will—can be hard work, especially when we use denial or blame to deal with our problems. But life gives us many opportunities to work on them, revisiting them again and again until we face the truth about ourselves and take charge of our lives.

PRACTICE WITH REFRAMING

To help you practice reframing, a practical exercise about an employee and her boss is presented below. I've included a step-by-step description of how to correctly reframe the pieces of the story. As you work with this exercise, you may wish to refer back to earlier chapters in the book.

EXERCISE: CAROL & WESLEY
CREATING A COMPLETE PICTURE & A DIFFERENT PERSPECTIVE

Here is the description an employee, Carol, wrote about her ex-boss, Wesley. After you review the information that is supplied, see how the picture can be reframed in order to better understand the situation between this man and woman. Is Carol looking at the entire "elephant" or just part of it?

> *"Wesley was stressed out and frustrated a lot. He always felt that women were disorganized and spacey. If he couldn't see it, it didn't exist. He needed proof for everything, and he always had to know all the details. He didn't share much about himself. Most of the time, he talked from his head instead of his heart. He was a penny pincher. He loved the fact that his checkbook was always balanced to the penny. Another thing he loved was the computer. He had an annoying habit of flipping a coin in his hand when he talked to me. I always felt belittled around him. I left my job because of him."*

What can you put together about Wesley and Carol with the information you now know about the mind, heart, and body? See if you can identify the following pieces of this picture:

- What is Wesley's learning style? Left or right hemisphere?
- What is his processing pattern?
- Which of the four control techniques does he use?
- What are his beliefs?
- Why would Carol find him to be irritating?

STOP!

Before you read my evaluation of Wesley, write down the answers to the questions above and see how you put the pieces together. Then, imagine you are Carol and reframe the picture!

Wesley's Profile

LEARNING STYLE

He's left-hemisphere dominant; he likes details, structure, logic, and organization.

PROCESSING PATTERN

Visual-Kinesthetic-Auditory
- He is not a talker.
- He uses his kinesthetic sense by flipping a coin when he talks with others.
- He needs to see something to believe it.
- He is a concrete learner.
- He loves computers (VKAs are usually great on computers.)

CONTROL TECHNIQUE

Accuser/Shielder

BELIEFS

- Woman are disorganized.
- You can't trust what you can't see.

SUMMARY

Wesley is very uncomfortable with someone he doesn't understand. He expects everyone to be organized. He is a very intelligent man who likes to control people by belittling them. He isn't into small talk, and he feels uncomfortable allowing employees to get to know him outside of the office. To trust, he needs to feel safe, and he can't put his faith in abstract concepts. His world is safe when it is organized and he is in control. He fears loss of control when he gets too close to someone.

Now, here is how Wesley described Carol. Again, is Wesley looking at the entire "elephant" or just part of it?

"Carol was a chatterbox. I found it very irritating how she always had to know everyone else's business. She also had a problem with organization. Her desk was always a mess, covered with papers and things. I think she was too busy trying to save the world and make everyone happy to get her work done. She was the one who seemed to plan all the social events in the office. I think she liked the attention. I never knew if I could trust her, since she wouldn't look me in the eye when I spoke to her. She was a very nervous woman— always meddling in others' affairs. I think she had a problem with men."

Carol's Profile

LEARNING STYLE
She's right-hemisphere dominant. She doesn't feel that the world needs to be organized all the time, but she also feels uncomfortable and judged by others when she is disorganized.

PROCESSING PATTERN
Auditory-Kinesthetic-Visual
- She likes to talk a lot.
- She isn't consciously aware that her workplace is not neat and tidy.
- She is very emotional and can easily express her emotions.

CONTROL TECHNIQUE
Shielder/Accuser/ Whiner—She becomes insulated and withdrawn whenever she feels like she is being put down and can't think for herself.

BELIEFS

- It is good to be open and share with people.
- People who can't share aren't to be trusted.
- If people don't like me, they don't talk to me.

SUMMARY

Carol is very sociable and is uncomfortable with a life that is too organized. She doesn't feel comfortable around a person who reminds her of her inability to be organized. She is very outgoing and creative, and she believes that people who don't open up to her don't like her. She doesn't trust people who keep things from her. Her world is safe when she knows about everything she can't control. She needs to feel needed and close to people to feel like she has worth.

Wesley and Carol found each other to be a challenge because they reflected back to each other the parts of themselves about which they feel inadequate. Thus, out

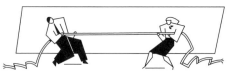

of fear, they created a tug-of-war over control. Carol ended up leaving.

In the Appendix on pages 215–219 there are four other stories involving Ben, Jill, Dean, and Judy. See how you do putting those pieces together into complete pictures.

JUDGMENT & REFRAMING

What does the exercise about Wesley and Carol teach us? Among other things, that they both were firmly stuck in their own world views! They were triggering each other's reactive brain, and neither was able to reframe their view of the other.

In many cases, it is because of our insecurities that we have a difficult time understanding other people—and end up making negative judgments about them.

■ *Case Study #34: The Homecoming Queen*

Once, when I was in my twenties, I sat next to a very striking woman who was about the same age, watching

a tennis tournament. I had heard that she was a
former college homecoming queen. Whenever I tried to
talk to her, she only responded with a yes or no answer.
I figured she was a stuck-up snob and wrote her off. If
she didn't like me, then I'd just avoid her.

Later, after life threw us together in many
situations, we got to be good friends. She shared with
me how nervous she was that day. She said that she
thought I was much smarter than she was; she felt
stupid and couldn't think of anything to say. When
she told me this, she helped me to understand how I
had prejudged someone based on my own insecurities.
It turned out she was a KVA and I was an AVK!

All too often, I see teachers and employers making
the same mistake in our schools and workplaces. A KVA
student or employee who spaces out and daydreams
while someone is speaking may be considered lazy, rude,
or indifferent by a teacher or boss. Most are not. Trying to
stay focused on lectures and not moving their bodies
makes them uncomfortable and tired, but they are *not* all
lazy or indifferent.

If you are speaking, and you see a person falling
asleep or daydreaming, you may think that person is
being rude, showing off, or trying to get at you by using
an attitude of boredom. This person could very well be a
kinesthetic-dominant processor who is auditorily re-
pressed. Or perhaps he is an exhausted student who
stayed up all night taking care of an ailing parent. (One
teenager was too afraid to let anyone know that his only
parent, his father, had an alcohol problem. The teen let
his teacher believe that he was just lazy when he fell
asleep in class; that way, he could avoid telling her that
he was up all night taking care of his father.)

Instead of jumping to conclusions and writing
someone off, we need to take the time to understand
what our snap judgments are based upon. Then we can
reframe our picture of that person. The following case
study illustrates what a difference this can make in
someone's life.

■ Case Study #35: Reframing Ben

Ben's math teacher approached me because she was concerned about Ben falling asleep in class and flunking math. Ben, a KAV processor, had math the last hour of the day. His teacher used the chalkboard a lot in her teaching. Ben had a very difficult time staying focused. He couldn't recall what his teacher explained in class because he kept falling asleep.

When he was allowed to use techniques that involved large muscle movement, Ben was able to recall his math work and understand its concepts and processes. His teacher agreed to allow him to sit at the end of the aisle where he could stretch his legs out and stand up; then he was able to stay focused on his work. He also caught up by going back over the first chapters and reviewing the material using his own learning techniques.

Because Ben's teacher wanted to understand his behavior instead of judging him, she was very supportive and open to helping Ben use his own method of learning. She was able to reframe her initial picture of him. As a result, Ben received a high grade on his final comprehensive math test.

Here is another situation in which reframing an initial impression made a difference—in this case, to a company.

■ Case Study #36: Swivel Chair Input

An employer, named Al, was upset and disappointed with a new employee, Ken. Al said that Ken didn't take team meetings seriously because he was always closing his eyes and not listening. Al liked him and thought he was a good worker, but he just couldn't accept Ken's "bad attitude" at the team meetings.

Ken was a KVA, and he had a difficult time staying awake when he sat too long in a meeting at the end of the day. As an auditorily unconscious (Level 3) processor, it was difficult for him to stay focused on what was being said unless his muscles were involved and he held a visual in his hand. Ken found the meetings to be long and boring, and he usually chose to space out rather than sit still for over an hour trying to listen.

After Al agreed to allow Ken to sit in a swivel chair, where he could rotate his body back and forth while he listened, the problem was solved. Al noticed that Ken not only stayed alert, but that he gave valuable input at the meetings.

To reframe our picture of another person, we need to consider all the pieces of the picture: hemispheric dominance, processing patterns, control techniques, fears, and beliefs. We may not know all of this information about someone else, but just knowing that every person has a unique mix of all these variables can help us to judge others less quickly.

REFRAMING OURSELVES

In addition to being able to reframe our picture of others, it is just as (or even more) important that we be willing to reframe our view of ourselves. We can become stuck in our fears and choose to project our problems onto others instead of "owning our stuff." **But once we take responsibility for ourselves, we have the power to change what we don't like.** Let's look at how this plays out in education.

Too often, students will be so defeated by their experiences in school that they just give up trying. I have seen many KVAs and KAVs who have the passion to play basketball or football declared ineligible because of their grades. For many of them, participating in a sport is the only reason they keep going to school. Their dream of getting into college with a scholarship is shattered when they can't play sports.

Many gang members I've worked with originally wanted to be athletes; they quit school because they

> "We must believe that we are gifted for something, and that this thing, at whatever cost, must be obtained."
>
> — Marie Curie, Scientist

couldn't make the grade. Most of them were highly kinesthetic and had a hard time sitting still. Some of them struggled with visual skills, such as writing and reading. They were all very coordinated physically. But their report cards inevitably had statements like: "not turning in work," "too many incompletes," and "flunking tests." Obviously, these students had a lot of red flags. Unfortunately, they also fell between the cracks and were mislabeled as lazy or irresponsible.

The pain caused by having one's dreams crushed can last for a very long time. Some adults, who have similar stories about their ineligibility for high school sports, still carry grudges and blame those who "took my dream away." Years later, they may still have a hard time believing in the future and find it difficult to keep a job. The bottom line is that these individuals need to let go of their victim attitude, reframe their thinking about their abilities, and focus on their future.

> It is always possible to change your life if you choose to find success.

It is always possible to change your life if you choose to find success. The first step is to reframe your self-portrait. Start by suspending your negative thoughts. Create a positive, clear visual image for your subconscious mind. See, hear, and/or feel yourself living the type of life you choose to live. Do this every day. Keep at it. You will begin to see things change. At the same time, get involved with helping others to find success and happiness. When you do, success and happiness will find you.

The next case study describes Kenny, someone who reframed his self-portrait and is achieving his goals.

■ *Case Study #37: Kenny*

Kenny, a very talented basketball player, was declared ineligible to play sports because of his math and reading grades. He was strongly right hemispheric and he had the classic problem of a KAV—difficulty recalling and imprinting visual information if he couldn't move his large muscles. His teachers wrote him off, judged him as lazy, and gave him detentions for not completing his work or turning it in on time. Kenny was uncomfortable going up and asking for help because he thought he was stupid.

When the teachers took away his eligibility to play basketball, they took away his passion and dreams. Believing that he was one of life's victims and that nothing good would ever happen to him, he quit school and started hanging out on the street with a gang.

After several incidents in which he made poor choices, Kenny eventually came to our center for help. When he realized that he could learn and that he was smart, he decided to go for his GED. Today he is attending college.

Kenny believed that he was stupid and that nothing good in life would ever come to him. This kept him in a victim mind frame. It wasn't until he took the risk of working on his math and reading skills that he began to see himself as worthy and capable of success. No one could do the reframing process for him. Yet, with help and encouragement from others, Kenny was able to trust himself. He eventually changed his belief from "I don't deserve to have good things happen in my life" to "I am good enough and I deserve the happiness I create."

FRIENDS: HELP WITH REFRAMING

Sometimes, we need a safe place to learn to risk again and trust ourselves. And sometimes friends or mentors can help us reframe our self-portrait and positively influence our path in life. This was the case with my friend Rudy Lawson, who is internationally known as "Mr. Rudy the Edu-tainer."

Although Rudy had a 1.7 grade point average, he was able to go to college because of his athletic skills and a Martin Luther King, Jr. Minority Program Scholarship. But when he went to college, he still relied on his old belief system—the street smarts he had used for so long for survival. After spending many years trying to be "smart enough" to be successful, he just couldn't trust the fact that he was good enough without his street survival tactics.

Rudy likes to share the following story in order to help people understand how a good person who is caught in a victim mindset can benefit from a helping hand.

■ *Case Study #38: Rudy's Story*

Rudy believes that he owes much to a special college coach who served as his mentor and guide at the time he reached a turning point in his life. Rudy needed money, and he devised a plan to hold up a pizza delivery boy with an unloaded gun. He remembers actually believing that it was a very good plan, since he didn't intend to hurt the boy. He was proud that he was able to come up with an easy and clever way to get some money.

As a KAV, Rudy struggled with cause and effect. He was very impulsive, and he didn't think about the possible negative outcomes of his plan. Fortunately, he talked to his coach about his plan before he actually went through with it. His coach patiently pointed out the problems with the plan, and Rudy listened to him. If Rudy hadn't shared his plan with his coach and listened to his guidance, his future might have headed in a very different direction.

In this case, Rudy's admiration for and trust in his coach helped him refrain from making the wrong decision. Rudy didn't change his beliefs about himself overnight, but because his coach believed in him, he started believing in himself. He began to work on turning his life around.

When you believe it, you will see it!

Today, Rudy has a teaching degree, which allows him to help millions of youth with his "I AM SMART" multisensory program. His wonderful talent for singing and writing songs around multisensory curricula helps youth believe in themselves and find success in life. (More information about Rudy Lawson is included in the Appendix on page 226.)

TEACHING OURSELVES

Every one of us is just a thought away from changing our lives. It's all about choice. When you change your beliefs, you change your experiences. This, in turn, helps you reframe your picture of life. You can create the life you choose by believing that you can have it and that you deserve it. Instead of saying, "I think I can," say instead, "I know I can"…and you will!

> **Every one of us is just a thought away from changing our lives. It's all about choice.**

Let me caution you about one thing. The reframing process is very powerful, but it is not a quick fix or an overnight transformation. Although some people experience sudden insights and shifts in their view of things, for most of us this is an ongoing process. We will continue to work on it throughout our lives.

CHAPTER 9
INDIVIDUALS,
ORGANIZATIONS
& CHANGE

■ ■ ■

"If we can find meaning in work,
we can keep ourselves recharged,
and the organizations
we work for stand a chance of
staying renewed themselves."

∽ Robert H. Waterman ∽
AUTHOR

Up to this point we have been exploring individuals—what makes us who we are, what we believe, and how we relate to each other one-on-one. But we do not exist as individual beings in a vacuum.

...just as every individual living organism has its own life energy, our organizations and groups also have energy.

Humans are a social species, from both necessity and pleasure. We gather in organizations, groups, and teams for survival, to get something done, and to have fun. And just as every individual living organism has its own life energy, our organizations and groups also have energy. After all, a group—whether it's a school, a company, or a family—is a gathering of individuals.

For an organization or team of any kind to be healthy, balanced, and productive, the people involved need to trust one another, share a purpose or goal, and be able to communicate effectively with each other. If one or more of the group's members are fearful or dysfunctional, it negatively affects the whole organization.

THE INDIVIDUAL MATRIX

To understand how organizations and their members operate, let's start by looking at two different models for how humans approach health, growth, and happiness.

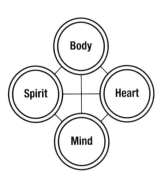

The first model focuses on function and is somewhat mechanistic. In this view, the body, mind, heart, and spirit are seen as connected but separate parts; they each need to be healthy and functional in order to keep the entire system running. If a part has a problem, it should be corrected so that the difficulty won't spread and/or affect the rest of the system. In medical terms, this usually means medication, surgery, or some other form of therapy.

In the second model, humans are viewed as a highly integrated matrix system involving the mind, body, heart, and spirit. Although each of the components has its separate purpose, they all are interdependent. No one part is any more or any less important than another, and they all contribute to the functioning, balance, and well-being of the whole system. Thus, if a person has a particular problem, he/she needs to heal more than just the organ(s) involved. Instead, the entire matrix of the individual needs to be addressed, including the beliefs, emotions, and thought processes that caused the system to become imbalanced in the first place.

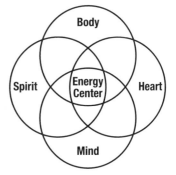

THE ORGANIZATIONAL MATRIX

The same two models can be applied to any group or organization. Every organization has its own mind, body, heart, and spirit. For example, let's use a business.

In the first model, the organization is structured along the lines of a traditional hierarchy. The mind of the company is made up of the top administrators and the board of directors. The body of the company refers to the employees—the people who create the products or services and do the work. The heart of the company can be seen in what all of its people feel about the organization, its customers or clients, and its products or services. The spirit of the company is the most intangible; it involves what people believe about the organization and its purpose or mission.

Under this structure, the administrators (mind) make decisions and relay the information down to the employees (body), who react but have little input into the decisions. People's feelings (heart) and beliefs (spirit) are acknowledged to exist, but may be considered unimportant or even a hindrance to "getting the work done."

In the United States, some variation of the second model—that of an integrated matrix—is being adopted by an increasing number of businesses. This change in our companies reflects a revised understanding of how individuals operate.

In this model, decision-makers (mind) are interwoven throughout the structure of the company, with people from all parts of the organization encouraged to contribute and become involved in the decision-making process. The employees (body) take responsibility for the success and well-being of the entire organization. Out of necessity, this involves everyone's feelings and beliefs (heart and spirit) about themselves, their product or service, their customers, and the company's mission.

INDIVIDUALS & PRODUCTIVE ORGANIZATIONS

In one sense, it does not matter how an organization is structured. If any part is unhealthy or disconnected, the entire system becomes weak and disrupted. Whether you're dealing with an individual, a company or school, a sports team, or a governmental entity, you're still working with the communication of the mind, body, heart, and spirit.

To maintain a healthy and productive organization, every person and every department must be able to communicate its needs by continually sharing information with others.

To maintain a healthy and productive organization, every person and every department must be able to communicate its needs by continually sharing information with others. Each person is valuable and contributes to the survival of the entire system. One unhappy, fearful, angry, or bored person or unit can block the organization's productivity and create havoc throughout the system. A business, school, or family can only be as successful as its weakest link; everyone involved needs to be committed to its goals and able to communicate with each other.

I began this book with a formula for success: **Passion + Vision + Action = Success. This applies not just to individuals, but to groups as well.** Every organization must have all three of these ingredients to achieve success. Missing any one of the three results in organizational struggle. But when a group of people comes together to support a need or vision they feel they can fulfill, they cannot be stopped.

The following exercise is called "Organizational Health Checkup." It contains some questions that will help you evaluate the well-being of any organization, group, or team.

EXERCISE: ORGANIZATIONAL HEALTH CHECKUP

The questions below can help you evaluate the status of your organization's overall health. You can use this to explore the dynamics of any group, whether it's a business, social organization, family, school, or governmental unit.

1. How healthy is your organization's "mind"?
   - What kind of self-talk do members engage in?
   - What are their dominant beliefs?
   - How are members trying to control things? Are these attempts constructive? Destructive?
   - How well are the leaders sharing information with the rest of the members?

2. How healthy is your organization's "body"?
   - Are the individual members healthy and productive?
   - Are the members communicating with one another effectively?
   - Are everyone's needs being met?
   - Are there any blocks to the flow of information, services, tools, products, etc.?

3. How healthy is your organization's "heart"?
   - Do the members feel nurtured and support one another?
   - Are members able to freely give and receive their time, talents, ideas, hopes, concerns, etc.?
   - Is anyone storing unexpressed fear, anger, or grief?

4. How healthy is your organization's "spirit"?
   - Does the organization have a vision about its mission? Do the members share that vision?
   - Does the organization have a passion? What is it? Do the members share that passion?
   - What actions are the members taking to bring the vision into reality? What do they need to be doing?

5. On a scale of 1-10, with 1 being nearly dead and 10

being radiantly healthy, how healthy is your whole organization?

6. Is there anything you would prescribe for the organization?

YOU ARE WHERE YOU CHOOSE TO BE

Do you love your work? The organization you work for? The people you work with? The product or service you provide? If not, are you contributing to the health of the organization or creating a problem? Be honest with yourself. Would you rather be somewhere else doing something else? If so, think about this: because an organization is only as strong as its least secure link, you are not doing yourself or the company any favors by staying where you do not want to be.

Perhaps you don't know how you feel about your work. Or maybe you have mixed feelings and you're not sure which is strongest. In the Appendix on page 220 is an exercise that will help you sort through this. It's called "Your Work: Why Are You Here?" If you would like to have a clearer sense of your thoughts, beliefs, and feelings about your work, do that exercise before you continue reading.

When I hear employees say things like, "I hate my job," or "I hate working here," I ask them why they continue to stay where they are not happy. The typical reply is one of the following statements:

- "I need the work."
- "I need to support my family."
- "I've been here a long time; I'm getting close to retirement."
- "I haven't gotten around to finding another job."

They usually aren't happy when I respond, "Then you are where you really want to be"! But after they think about it, they can see the truth behind this statement.

If we really want to change something in our lives, we will create change by taking action. As you may recall from the first chapter, people who have passion plus vision without action are dreamers. They think, "Someday I plan to…" or "I really wish that I could…" They believe that something or someone else is responsible for their situation—and is keeping them from taking action.

Most people stay where they are for two reasons: they're afraid to let go of what they have, and/or they're afraid of what they may lose if they let go. Change brings out our fears. Some people would rather settle for being unhappy in a situation they know rather than create change in their lives. If you *really* want to find another job, get out of a relationship, move to another place, or try out for a team, you will put out the effort needed to make your desire come true...unless, of course, your fear is greater than your desire.

> Most people stay where they are for two reasons: they're afraid to let go of what they have, and/or they're afraid of what they may lose if they let go.

Such fear is usually based on a deep feeling of low self-esteem. This can lead people to remain stuck in relationships and jobs that they have outgrown. **When people choose to hang on to—and act out of—their fears, they show that they trust these fears more than they trust themselves.** This belief can be so strong that individuals will convince themselves that they deserve to have negative things happen to them. (Refer back to Case Study #27: Abuse On The Bus on page 125 for an example of this.)

Low self-esteem can cause people to trust their negative beliefs so much that they will defend those negative beliefs no matter what. They seem to need to prove to the world that it doesn't matter what they do, it won't work out. These individuals will continually set themselves up to fail in order to prove that they are right about being failures! They may make comments like the following: "See, I told you I would flunk," or "I told you that it wouldn't work out. Now do you believe me?"

Although it doesn't sound logical on the surface, we gain something from carrying negative beliefs and attitudes toward ourselves and others. And we will continue to feed our negative beliefs until we no longer need what we

> ...we gain something from carrying negative beliefs and attitudes toward ourselves and others.

gain from them. However, once we are aware of this dynamic, we can choose to let the negative beliefs go.

How do we do this? To begin with, we need to validate our feelings and be willing to let go of our inner judgments about ourselves. Look at the next case study.

■ *Case Study #39: Putting Out Fires*

> *Kyle was an expert at putting out fires—not those with flames and smoke, but "hot" situations that involved people. As he described his life, he said, "I have to put out fires everywhere I go. I'm getting tired of it." When asked why he seemed to be the only one available to handle these situations, he replied, "I guess I'm the only one who can do it."*
>
> *What Kyle didn't see was that he was always putting out fires and fixing situations because he believed that he needed to save or fix something in order to feel worthwhile. His self-esteem was linked to fixing others' problems. Even though he complained about putting out fires, he was exactly where he wanted to be when they erupted.*
>
> *As Kyle learned to let go and trust in his own worth as a person, he began to focus on taking care of his own needs. Then he was able to let go of his need to save others. Instead of trying to be everyone's savior, he got involved in activities like golf and baseball where he felt accepted and enjoyed being just another member of the group.*

This same belief is in play when someone chooses to stay in a bad relationship in order to satisfy the need to be the "healthy" one who can fix the other person. "He needs me to take care of him," is really based on the belief, "When I am the healthiest one, I am needed and loved."

The next time you find yourself complaining about a situation in which you are involved, ask yourself, "Why am I still here?" Are you working on getting out? Your answers will show what you really believe.

Remember, there is no wrong or right in your decision to get out of or stay in a particular situation. It is your choice, which is based on what you are gaining from the experience. (Perhaps complaining is a way to remind yourself that you have a choice!)

Right now, you are where you choose to be. So whether you are a student whose job is to get an education, an employee working in a large company, or a parent raising children, the bottom line is, "Take your job and love it!" Or get to work on changing things.

ORGANIZATIONAL TRANSITION & FEAR

All organizations go through transitions. With transition comes change, which normally generates fear. Any company undergoing change will see its employees act out of these fears—the fear of losing a job, taking a cut in pay, being forced to do a different job, having to retrain, and so on. These are just a few examples of the experiences that cause employees to feel angry. **Change is almost always painful, but it is *always* an opportunity for growth.** The next two case studies show this.

■ *Case Study #40: Laid Off & Loving It*

Kirby was a skilled manager who had worked with a company for over 35 years when he was laid off during a corporate merger. Although the severance package was adequate, he was terrified that he was too old to find another company that would want his skills. He was also very angry at being treated so poorly by the company to which he had given so much for so long. He had almost sacrificed his marriage to his work, and had lost precious years while his sons were growing up.

When Kirby let go of his victim attitude and decided to focus on creating what he wanted for his next job, he was open for a new opportunity. It came quickly. Within the same year, he found a completely new kind of job with flexible hours, better pay, and more paid vacation time. It was exactly what he wanted. Looking back, he now considers it a blessing that the other company let him go.

Another illustration of change and opportunity involves an employee who was transferred to another part of her employer's facilities.

■ *Case Study #41: The Transfer*

During a corporate down-sizing, Berty was given the choice of being laid off or moving to another unit in the company. If she stayed, she would need to be retrained. She decided to stay. But even after completing her training, she was still very angry; she believed that the company was actually trying to get rid of her.

When Berty finally decided to let go of her anger and make the best of the situation, she started to have ideas for improving the production line's efficiency, which she shared with her supervisor. Six months later, when her supervisor retired, Berty was promoted to that position and given a large raise. Her supervisor recommended her for his position because he was so impressed with her work record, initiative, and attitude.

Sometimes we are forced to change through a catastrophe that appears to come out of nowhere. Often, this has to do with the organizations or groups with which we are involved. The next case study, one of my own experiences, shows that the "group" may be very small but the impact very large!

■ *Case Study #42: Embezzlement*

I had the opportunity to learn first-hand about deception and loss when a man I employed as my marketing manager embezzled a large amount of money. My first reaction, of course, was that of a victim. "Why me? Why is life after me?"

It wasn't until much later that I realized the valuable lesson he taught me. If he hadn't embezzled the money from me and bounced checks all over Florida, I would never have left the safety of my teaching career. Because of the embezzlement, I was forced to take a year's leave of absence from the classroom to save my name and my meager audiotape business. I ended up creating what I thought would be a temporary learning center—a place of refuge for just that year until I straightened out my tape business and returned to the classroom.

In the long run, it all turned out for the best. He paid back most of the money without a criminal record and I learned one of the most valuable lessons a businesswoman can learn—to always keep a strong thumb on the pulse of my business. I forgave him and myself, and I still thank him for teaching me that lesson.

Many years have gone by since this occurred. I now consider the money I lost as my investment in a much higher education. I had given my power away to another person because I was afraid I couldn't create a business myself. I chose security over pursuing my passion—until I was forced by circumstances to make the changes that I really wanted to make all along!

This is not unusual. We may help create a powerful (and perhaps painful) lesson in order to grab our own attention and get ourselves back on track. In this case, my fear of losing financial security kept me from pursuing my passion. The act of embezzlement forced me to deal with this fear and let go long enough to go after what I really wanted.

Whenever your work or your personal life is undergoing some type of transition, you have the opportunity to grow. As frightening as this can be, life becomes stagnant without change. Look back on your life and recall the changes you have already lived through. You have already faced fear, and you are stronger than you may think.

When you let go of fear and allow yourself to trust life, you can welcome transition as a positive experience and be ready for the new opportunities that are coming. So embrace change and look for the opportunity hidden behind your fear.

...embrace change and look for the opportunity hidden behind your fear.

WHERE ARE YOU GOING?

For now, you are where you really want to be. What comes next?

- First, you need to know what your passion is.

■ Second, you need to understand, as clearly and completely as possible, where you are right now and where you want to go.

■ Finally, you need to define your plan for success—how you're going to get there.

FIRST…

Following is an exercise called "Discovering Your Passion." Start with that.

EXERCISE: DISCOVERING YOUR PASSION

There are many ways to explore and discover what you care about passionately. This one takes you back to look at what you've always loved.

1. Get a piece of paper and write down all the things you enjoyed doing in your childhood.
2. Turn the paper over and write down all the things you love to do today.
3. Circle all the activities that you love to do today that are also on your list of childhood activities.
4. Put a star beside each of the circled activities you have done in the past year.
5. Put a second star next to the activities you have done in the past month.

The activities you put on your childhood list may be a key to discovering or unlocking your passion. How many of your favorite childhood activities are included in your life today? How often do you do them? The closer you are to the child you were, the closer you are to your passion.

For example, if you loved to play school as a child, you may find that your passion is teaching. If you loved to take things apart to see what made them tick, your passion may be in the field of engineering or mechanics. If you loved to sing, you may find that your passion is connected to being a choir director or a singer.

Remember: your vocation—what you feel called to do or what you are passionate about—may not necessarily be how you make your living. Don't feel you need to cram your passion into a job description! A woman I know makes her living as a secretary. But she has a beautiful voice and is passionate about music. She is part of a vocal trio that travels throughout the United States and Europe during holidays, weekends, and vacations, singing the music they love. She is definitely living her passion!

SECOND...

Now use the next exercise, called "The Part You Play," to understand more about where you are now and where you would like to go.

EXERCISE: THE PART YOU PLAY

Use this exercise to help clarify your current situation and decide where you would like to go. Although it is designed with the workplace in mind, you can use this exercise in relation to any group you're involved with—family, social club, religious organization, etc.

Today...
1. What part do you play in your current workplace?
2. Why are you there?
3. How does being there affect your life? Is it mostly negative or positive?
4. Are your physical, emotional, mental, and spiritual needs being met?
5. How do you affect where you are? Do you think you are a positive or a negative influence?
6. What are you learning by being there?
7. What are you teaching others by being there?

Tomorrow...
1. What are your hopes and dreams involving your current work?
2. What can you gain from staying in your current situation?
3. What might you gain from doing something else or going somewhere else?
4. What can your workplace gain if you stay in your current situation?
5. How well does your current work fit with your passion?
6. How does where you are now fit into your plan for the future?

FINALLY...YOUR PLAN FOR SUCCESS

Once you understand where you are now and where you want to go, it is time to start creating your plan for success. To begin, you need to decide very specifically what it is that you want to create in your life. Even though your plan will change many times, having one will help you begin working toward what you choose to create.

Why have a plan at all? When you create your personal success plan, you are giving your subconscious mind a blueprint to work from. Whenever you write down your thoughts or say them out loud, they are imprinted more vividly in your mind. And the more clearly you experience (see, hear, feel) what is imprinted in your mind, the easier it becomes to manifest what you want in your life.

HOW TO CREATE A PLAN

Creating a plan for success does not have to be complicated or time-consuming, but you should use a process that matches the way your brain handles detailed information.

Some people are "big-picture" types. They understand things better if they can get an overview of what they're trying to do first, and then fill in the details later. These individuals need to see the forest before they can make sense of the trees. Others are conceptual builders. They need to see the details (the individual trees) before they can make sense of the big picture (the forest).

The process outlined below is likely to be most comfortable for conceptual builders. If you would rather start with the big picture, you may want to develop an overview of some kind first. For example, you can write a vision statement, draw a picture, create a mind-map, compose a piece of music, lay out a representation in physical space, or do anything else that will help you see/hear/feel your goal.

PLANNING FOR SUCCESS: A PROCESS

Here is a seven-step process to help you start constructing your blueprint for success. Don't feel that you need to begin with something as profound as your life's purpose. You can start with something small—like taking a trip, starting a garden, or getting an apartment.

One other thing to note. Although step #7 describes a way to share your plan with others, you don't need to share this plan—or even that you have created a plan—with anyone else unless you choose to do so. It's your life. It's your plan.

1. Identify a specific goal. Your goal must be for you. Do not choose something for a friend or relative, i.e., something that you believe someone else wants you to do. This is your goal, and it's going to be your success.

2. Write your goal down in as much detail as you can. Include a time frame, even if it's very loose at this point.

3. Write down why you want to achieve this goal. What will you gain? Be ruthlessly honest with yourself. Don't put down a reason because you think it sounds better or more profound than the real reason. The real reason—whatever it is—is good enough.

4. Write down the obstacles you think you may face, along with possible ways they can be overcome.

5. Take action toward achieving the goal by gathering any missing information and investigating all of your options.

6. Focus on your goal. See it as if it has already happened. Cut out pictures and place them in front of you. Include as much color, emotion, and movement as you can when you imagine yourself reaching your goal.

7. Share your goal with a few people, but only those who will be supportive. Choose those people wisely. Once your subconscious mind hears a negative judgment from someone whose opinion you value, it can block your success.

BUT DOES IT WORK?

Does planning for success work? Yes! I followed these steps years ago when I wanted to create a learning center. After going through each of these steps and mapping a strategy for how I was going to reach my goal, I began to visualize it coming together. I started my plan in January 1991; I opened my first center in March. That was just three months later!

When I share this story, people assume that I already had the money. I didn't. But I was able to find a way to have the program financed without the help of a bank. I also had to somehow find a building that was almost rent-free. That happened. Finally, I had to create a program that would attract the children who were struggling in school and needed special help. I did. But I didn't do it alone.

The more challenges you overcome, the more exhilarating it will be when you reach your goal.

After many years, it is still amazing to me to see how the right people and circumstances "just happen" to appear at the right time when someone is truly focused on his/her passion. I have experienced this type of support repeatedly. The phrase from the movie *Field of Dreams* is true: "If you build it, they will come."

You will have countless opportunities to be resourceful and work around obstacles, but you will find success. The more challenges you overcome, the more exhilarating it will be when you reach your goal. There is one catch to all this. Once you see that you can create what you imagine, your creations will grow bigger and bigger!

In the Appendix on page 223 is an exercise called "Creating Your Plan For Success." Turn to that now and start creating!

CHAPTER 10
THE GLOBAL PICTURE

■ ■ ■

"We are the dwelling place
of incredible opportunities.
They live in us.
…We can make it work.
We will make it work."

～ John Denver ～
SINGER & SONG-WRITER

Today the world faces fear in every possible direction. Conflicts, large and small, are being fought in almost every area of our lives. Battles rage not only between nations, but in our homes, communities, governments, neighborhoods, and schools.

Whenever I ask people in an audience to list the reasons for war, they cite greed, money, low self-esteem, and religion. The seed for all of these power struggles is fear. As we have seen, fear is part of our being in the world; it is built into our physiology as animals. Yet, the more we focus on fear, the stronger the fear grows, and the greater is our need to try to control things.

What would our world look like if we could experience fear and then let it go, choosing to focus on love and abundance instead?

What would our world look like if we could experience fear and then let it go, choosing to focus on love and abundance instead? What if we behaved as though we were all "good enough"? When we know that we have all we need, and when we see each other as good enough, then we don't feel the need to hurt ourselves or anyone else.

CAUSE & EFFECT

To heal our world, we have to heed the law of cause and effect. For every action there is a reaction. **What we put out always comes back toward us.** It is true for how we treat the Earth itself, as well as how we treat each other.

When we give, abundance comes back to us. When we take, something is taken from us. When we are chronically jealous or angry or spiteful, we draw the jealousy, anger, and spite of others. When we wish another person well, we draw the same experience into our lives. The more we focus on and surround ourselves with loving, positive, successful people and ideas, the more we will bring those attributes into our lives. By making only one change—focusing on the positive aspects of our lives instead of the negative—we can reshape our entire experience of living.

> By making only one change—focusing on the positive aspects of our lives instead of the negative—we can reshape our entire experience of living.

We all seek to find love and acceptance in our lives. It doesn't matter if we are wealthy or poor, smart or stupid, thin or fat. That's all comparative; all we want is to be accepted as good enough. All the dramas we create are just scenes in the performance we call Life. Humans are very good actors. We can play the part of any character so convincingly that even *we* believe the role we are playing is who we really are! Yet, we are much more than just our roles in life, and we can achieve great success when we believe in ourselves—the individuals behind the masks.

THE CAVE

I once toured a cave where they turned off all the lights toward the end of the tour in order to show us what pure darkness looked like. I couldn't see my hand in front of my face. I felt for a moment like I had disappeared into nothingness. I was glad that we could hear each other. Then I noticed how much more the people in the group were interacting with one another in the darkness. Part of it was for reassurance in the face of our shared primal fear of the dark. But it was more than that. We were laughing and friendly. Then, when the lights came back on, everyone went back to being quiet, clumped together in their same small groups.

As brief as this experience was, it had an impact on me that I have thought about often. What if we all could first meet each other in a cave of darkness, where the outside of a person couldn't be judged first? Then we would know each other from the "insides out." Perhaps we could eliminate many of our prejudices and judgments.

…& THE INTERNET

Recently I realized that we have created this cave-like meeting place through the technology of the Internet and

the World Wide Web. Millions of people spend hours communicating with individuals who they will never physically meet. Teens freely share ideas and advice with adults who are twice their age. Friendships are created around the world without age, gender, appearance, or race being an issue. When I see people in the same room hardly speaking to each other, I wonder how many of them reach out every night over the Internet to make contact with people they don't know.

The Internet is a safe medium that offers us the mask of anonymity—the ability to reach out to each other as equals and come out of our shells with little risk. This has both its good and bad sides, of course. On the one hand, two people who do not reveal their true identities can be close chat room friends and not be aware that one of them is the "enemy" who took away the other's homeland. On the other hand, some people present themselves through a fictitious self and become so wrapped up in it that they lose their sense of who they are. Or they end up hurting someone else. The Internet can help us openly connect and share information with one another, or it can be a retreat that helps us hide from reality. Just like life. Just like the cave.

What Do We Want?

Our future is ours for the making. The same process that helps us create successful futures as individuals will work at the collective level also. **When a group of people takes small, consistent actions toward a goal that they have vividly imagined achieving, they can create anything.** So what do we want? Will our schools, busi-nesses, and political systems meet the challenge for needed change?

- Will we create and implement programs that teach and promote self-worth, unity, and acceptance of one another?

- Will we create systems that allow us to share our talents with each other and encourage us to perform at our best—without our personal worth being judged?

- Will we develop teaching and training methods that take advantage of each individual's learning process?

- Will we be able to create environments that promote tolerance, diversity, and an understanding that we are all the same beneath our apparent individuality?

- Will we be able to make the mental and emotional switch needed to let go of fear—to face our choices and challenges as exciting opportunities to grow stronger, healthier, and more productive?

- Will we revise our beliefs and begin to view our "failures" as positive and necessary times in our growth process?

In other words, can families, schools, businesses, hospitals, governments, and society in general be seen as microcosms of the larger classroom of life, where we continue to learn about ourselves while caring about others?

The information in this book is not about fluff or soft skills. It's about the bottom line—having the ability to understand ourselves and communicate effectively with each other in every part of our lives. Ask yourself if the following statements are true.

- Our friends and families serve as our safe harbors, nurturing us and offering us unconditional understanding, love, and acceptance.

- Our educational, governmental, and health care institutions focus on supplying the best tools and environments, thereby meeting every individual's needs for physical, mental, emotional, and spiritual growth and development.

- Our businesses create positive work environments where employees are valued and treat each other with respect. This attitude serves as the backbone for each company's employee relations, customer service, and productivity.

Does this sound utopian? Probably. In any event, I suspect you'll agree with me that we have more work to do!

WHERE DO WE GO FROM HERE?

On the cover of this book, under the title, are the words, "Understand Why You Do What You Do. Take Charge Of Your Life." Now that you have read this book, do you understand why you do what you do?

You do what you do for at least three reasons:

- Because you are a human being with an integrated mind/body system.
- Because your beliefs, based upon love or fear, create the feeling that you need to do what you do.
- Because your experiences create opportunities for you to know and see more clearly your authentic self—who you are versus who you *believe* you are.

Throughout the ages, people have struggled with the fear of not having or being enough. No matter how much we advance, we still focus on blocking our full potential with our fears.

Consider for a moment the negative aspects of life. How many of them are connected to our fears? As we've seen, many of our fears are formed early in our lives, when we buy into others' negative beliefs. These beliefs become a part of who we believe we are and are continually fed by our actions. We act out these beliefs during "performances" on the "stages" set within our families, governments, businesses, and schools.

Since children mirror a society's belief systems, let's look at the type of performances that have been occurring on the stage of our schools compared to those occurring in the surrounding world. Within a span of less than 20 years, our newspaper headlines have gone from asking "Why Can't Johnny Read?" and "Why Is Johnny Failing?" to "What Makes Johnny Kill?" Now we have to pay attention to the writing on the chalkboard.

Since you have read this book, perhaps you can understand how extensive the repercussions of our fears can be as they collectively penetrate more deeply into every part of our society. I believe that many of the answers to the questions appearing on the classroom chalkboard and in our news headlines can be found in the chapters of this book.

It doesn't matter if you are a child or an adult—a doctor, student, merchant, mechanic, or homemaker. The criteria for creating a healthy, balanced, productive, and successful life are the same for all. As more people become aware of the pieces contained in the whole picture, we come closer to reaching our highest potential in life, both as individuals and in our organizations. To do this, we all need to understand and take responsibility for who we are and what we do.

Regardless of your reason for reading this book, you did. Now you have another choice or responsibility. I believe that a brighter future will evolve as people share their knowledge about why we do what we do with one another. I wish the best for all of you and leave you with that opportunity.

Why not you?

Epilogue:
Reflections On
The Bumblebee
& Dorothy

■ ■ ■

THE BUMBLEBEE

Consider the Bumblebee's dilemma:
*It is told that such are the aerodynamics
and wing-loading of the bumblebee that,
in principle, it cannot fly.*

—John Kenneth Galbraith

Since nobody told the Bumblebee that he can't fly, he doesn't know that he can't. So he just goes on with his life, doing the "impossible" every day.

**What do you want to happen in your life?
Who says your dream is impossible?**

DOROTHY'S JOURNEY

In *The Wizard Of Oz*, Dorothy is tossed by life's events (a tornado) over the rainbow. Her heart's desire is to return home to Kansas. On her journey to the wizard who will grant this wish, she meets the Scarecrow, who wants a brain; the Lion, who wants courage; and the Tin Man, who wants a heart. With the help of her three friends—the mind, body, and heart—she faces the Wicked Witch (her fears) and completes her journey, learning a lot about herself and life in the process. At the end of her journey, Dorothy learns her greatest lesson, "If I ever go looking for my heart's desire again, I won't look any further than my own backyard…"

**Today,
you can begin to create the life you choose to live.
Success resides within you.
You deserve it.**

If you've read this book, you know that you are creating your life moment to moment by what you think and believe and feel and act upon. Now, when you hear yourself saying, "Why is this happening to me?," you know the answer. It's your life, your responsibility, *and* your opportunity. So why not you?

What do you choose to create today?

Appendix

RESOURCE A

HELPFUL MULTISENSORY TECHNIQUES FOR TEACHERS

REMINDER

■ Left hemisphere-dominant learners are interested in ordered parts, process, and semantics. They need to see the details.

■ Right hemisphere-dominant learners are interested in expression and the flow of language. They need to see the whole picture to answer their "Why?" questions.

READING TECHNIQUES

■ Teach students a question-and-answer reading technique. Show them how they can mentally turn all headings and subheadings into questions and then read the text that follows as answers to those questions.

■ Use a green transparency over what is being read.

■ Have students sit on large balls as they read. Bouncing, swaying, and rocking movements can increase focus and memory.

■ Have students hold something in their hands when reading in order to help them stay focused on the material.

■ Use phrase sheets to increase fluency. Challenge students to read all of the phrases within a certain amount of time. For example:
  · saw the dog
  · ran to the house
  · over the green river

■ Have students read into a recorder to hear and correct their own mistakes. This helps them to become discerning readers.

■ Have students walk and read at the same time. When students are afraid that they can't read, walking helps to take away the fear and unblocks their thought process. This technique increases fluency and comprehension.

- Have the students close their eyes and direct them to see pictures in their minds as you read to them. This helps visually unconscious students practice using their visual sense internally for comprehension; it will carry over as they read to themselves.

- Use web mapping for students to organize the events, characters, etc. of a story.

- Cut up cartoons and ask students to put them in the correct sequence. This helps visually unconscious students to understand cause and effect. It also helps right hemisphere-dominant students to organize their thoughts.

- Use color shock. Separate compound words or syllables by color instead of spaces. Right hemisphere-dominant students need to see the whole picture before they process the parts. Using spaces to separate the words into syllables can confuse them.

- Have students sing sentences. This helps visually and auditorily unconscious students to stay focused on the information.

- Have students use different voices as they read. Using a foreign or regional accent helps them to stay focused on the material they are reading. They can also become characters, reading with their voice changed to match how the character might sound. (Little children love to read as if they were a dinosaur reading out loud.)

- Have students clap, walk, hop, jump, etc. as they read each word in the sentence. This helps kinesthetic children to slow down their minds and see the word order in sentences.

- When teaching spelling or vocabulary, "write" the words on the students' backs.

- Have students act out what they read.

- Have students touch their fingers to what they are reading (e.g., books, tests, computer screens) as their eyes scan down the page. This is known as "grounding." It helps visually unconscious processors with their anxiety before they take a test or read some text.

- Have kinesthetically dominant students touch all pictures and imagine what it would be like to feel each part of the picture as if it were real. This helps with visual recall.

- Have students circle consonant blends (i.e., bl, fl, gr) or vowels in newspaper articles or magazines within a certain amount of time. This helps them to move their eyes across the page and teaches them to be more discerning about how words begin and end.

A final technique for developing reading skills is called the **Warning Game**. This game helps students become more aware of their lazy reading habits. It can be played with an entire class or in a tutoring situation.

Have students read a paragraph out loud. If they make a mistake, say "Warning" after they come to the end of the sentence in which the mistake was made. If the students can find their mistake, they get a point. If they can't, you get a point.

When using this game in a group, divide the group into two teams. As one student reads, the other students have to pay very close attention so that they can help their teammate if the student who is reading asks for assistance. The student who is reading can choose to find his/her mistake or ask a teammate for help. If the student or teammate fails to find the mistake, the other team gets a chance to answer. Whichever team finds the mistake gets the point.

WRITING TECHNIQUES

- To teach writing to kinesthetic students, start with the large muscles first. Have them write large letters with their whole arm in the air, on a chalkboard, or on a large piece of paper as they close their eyes. It is important for them to have spatial awareness. Have them mimic the shape of letters with their bodies as they lay on the floor or stand up.

  Then have them make the same movements while their elbows are resting on the desk or floor. Have them write letters in the air. Continue to engage increasingly smaller muscles by using sand, paint, or a chalkboard. After they have good eye-hand control and spatial awareness, have them write on paper with a pencil.

- Use toothpaste to write letters or words on a table.

- Use sand or crushed noodles glued to paper in the shape of a letter. Have them close their eyes and trace the letters as they say the sounds.

MATH TECHNIQUES

1. First explain what you are going to teach them and why.
2. Create an overall picture. Tell them that you will go through the entire math problem first so they can see what it looks like before you break it down.
3. Go through the entire problem as you say your steps and thoughts out loud.
4. Next, go over the same problem step-by-step with your students.
5. Give them time to write each step down.
6. Supply another similar math problem for them to work on with you and at their desks.
7. Have them say the steps out loud with you as they mimic your actions. Have them teach the problems back to each other in a buddy situation.
8. Review with another similar problem on the board or overhead, and encourage your students to complete the problem. Supply an example of a problem that they already completed.

- Take the numbers out of story problems. Have your students see the story first. Act out the story, if possible, or draw a picture.

- Use manipulatives to teach math concepts; anything that can be held in their hands can be used. Get your students out of their chairs so they can use their large muscles as much as possible. For example, if you are teaching place values, have your students stand up in a line and give them each a card with a number on it. See if they can get their bodies in the correct order when you give them a number verbally.

- Always use the teach-back approach to imprint

your math lesson. Use charts and pictures as much as possible.

- Include large muscle movement, rhymes, raps, etc. to increase long-term recall.

- Have students jump and say math facts as they look at the factors. You can also use a trampoline, hula hoop, jump rope, or a cheerleader approach.

- Always include both the large and small muscles of the body. Be creative and make the lessons fun. This tends to be a scary subject for many visually and kinesthetically unconscious students.

STUDY SKILLS & FOCUSING

- Use lots of note cards in different colors. By using note cards and writing down key points from the information that they read, kinesthetic students who are visually unconscious will be able to study as they walk.

- Play Bach, Mozart, Beethoven, or Handel while they study. Certain kinds of Western classical music appear to increase the brain's ability to take in information.

- Allow students to take off their shoes. Kinesthetics seem to perform better on tests and stay focused longer on their work when their feet can feel the floor. Most of them take their shoes off as soon as they get home; it grounds them.

- Use a "Red Hot" folder for all assignment papers.
  - "Red Hot" means something is important and needs attention right away.
  - Visually unconscious students find notebooks with separate subject sections too confusing.
  - By using one folder, parents only have to check one place to see papers that are brought home.
  - It helps students to stop stuffing papers into books, where they usually get lost in the shuffle.
  - The folder should have a favorite design, sports team, music group, or hero on the cover. The more emotion that is attached to the folder, the better.

- Put the students who seem to have the hardest time staying focused on the aisle, where you can pat them on the back or touch their arms. They will come back from their day dreams when they are touched.

- Allow your kinesthetic students time to get drinks and move their large muscles. Some will perform better if they stand at a counter while they take tests.

- To help settle down young children, have them do somersaults or swing; do not have them spin.

- The Magic Lotion Technique is another good way to help little ones settle down. Have them pretend that they have a magic bottle of lotion that settles them down after they finish rubbing it all over their arms, legs, necks, and faces. This technique helps them to stimulate their neurological system in a controlled manner; it will calm them down.

- Encourage all of your students to drink water!!

THINKING SKILLS

- Have your students practice brain patterning exercises. An example of this is the command and repeat exercise. Tell the students a series of commands, then have them repeat those commands back to you exactly as you said them. If they say the commands correctly in the right order, they may perform the commands. For example, say, "Take three steps forward, turn left, put your left hand on your right hip, put your left hand on your right shoulder." Create longer and harder commands as they find the commands easier to master. This is an excellent exercise for all students who are struggling with their academic skills.

- Have students draw symmetrical pictures with each hand at the same time. Then have them draw asymmetrical pictures with each hand at the same time.

- Have students draw one picture with their left hand and another picture with their right hand at the same time.

- Have students draw a picture with their right hand and write a sentence with their left hand at the same time.

FOR ALL SUBJECTS & LEARNING ENVIRONMENTS

- Use kinesthetic, visual, and auditory techniques, including color, emotion, and movement in your lessons.

- Get your students up and moving every 15 or 20 minutes. Allow them to have frequent drinks of water or water bottles in the classroom.

- Always include the teach-back approach or a demo to lock in the information.

- Supply projects and tests that offer students with each processing pattern the ability to show or express what they know.

- Allow gum chewing (preferably sugarless!) if possible. It involves jaw movement, which stimulates the brain. This helps kinesthetic students stay focused and is especially helpful during stressful activities, such as tests.

COMMUNICATION SKILLS

- Remember: scared students would rather look "bad" than stupid to their peers. The more they strut, the greater their fear.

- A teacher who becomes a dictator or controller in order to maintain authority in his/her class will never actually have control.

- Students *want* to learn when they feel safe enough to risk.

- Teaching is the act of sharing your passion. Teachers don't turn the light on inside their students. They help their students discover the switch.

RESOURCE B

HELPFUL MULTISENSORY TRAINING TECHNIQUES FOR BUSINESSES

REMINDER

- Auditory processors need to say things out loud and teach back or demonstrate.

- Visual processors need to see charts, pictures, and color.

- Kinesthetic processors need to experience things through large and small muscle movements.

Include techniques that address all three processing styles—kinesthetic, visual, and auditory—as often as possible.

By incorporating the following suggestions through-out your business, you can meet every employee's needs.

- Post a visual flow chart that shows the relationship of all departments or work units and notes their tasks and responsibilities. This will help employees see the whole picture of the company and better understand and respect their position. (In a large company, many employees only know what their department does.)

- Post a visually interesting poster that describes the company's vision, mission, and goals.

- Use a teach-back approach and include kinesthetic techniques when training all employees.

- When tasks require small eye-hand movements or high stress, have employees take brief breaks every 20-30 minutes so they can relax their eyes from nearpoint focus.

- Allow employees to move and drink water at least every half hour.

- If possible, allow employees who choose to work to music to wear headphones.

- When training, break tasks down into parts. Make sure the employees understand the parts as well as the whole task.

- Do not assume that all employees can picture what is said. Visually unconscious processors may be reluctant to say that they don't understand something because they don't want to appear "stupid" in front of others.

- Use swivel chairs in meeting rooms for those who need to move to stay focused.

- Train the marketing staff to be familiar with all six processing patterns. This will help them learn how to approach and best serve each customer.

- Always use visuals and include some type of kinesthetic activity in your meetings. Some companies have discovered that placing skoosh balls on the table for kinesthetic employees is helpful.

- To make "reader friendly" written material, use a serif type face and large type. Break the material apart visually with spaces separating sections. Include visuals and color, such as line drawings, charts, graphs, and pictures.

- Have a visual agenda for any meeting, and go over it verbally before starting. This will help right hemispheric-dominant learners to feel less anxious and understand the whole picture.

- Use lightly colored green or yellow transparencies over computer screens to help employees' eyes.

- Offer both visual and auditory praise.

- Include the reasons for any changes in rules or procedures.

- Give employees time to figure numbers or compose written material. Never assume that an employee can add numbers or write what you need on the spot. (Even professional mathematicians and writers may not be able to produce "on the fly" if they are right-hemispheric dominant.)

COMMUNICATION SKILLS

If you remember and practice the following ideas, you will go a long way toward creating a happier, healthier, more productive workplace.

- People who are truly in control see the value in all employees and do not need to act controlling in order to be in control.

- Praise publicly and correct privately.

- Where there is anger, there is fear. Where there is fear, discover the belief behind it. Validate the fear and work on changing the belief.

- For a company to have success, it must see and treat every employee as an equally important part of the whole process. Lip-service to this idea is not enough.

- All company leaders need to promote and share their passion for the company's vision with all employees.

EXERCISE C

IDENTIFYING CLOSE ENERGY TAKERS

Get a piece of paper and trace around your hand. You are going to label each finger with the initials of the four people who are your current closest relationships. First, put your own initials in the middle finger. Then, on either side of that finger, place the initials of the two people whom you consider to be closest to you.

Now, as you read each of the following 17 statements, decide which person best fits each one. Write an "X" on the finger representing that person. A statement may not seem to apply to any of the people you've selected, or you may feel that a statement fits two people equally well. Try to select the one person who fits the statement best, and you will end up with a total of 17 "X" marks scattered somewhere on the fingers.

- The person who is most like you.
- The person who has the same values as you.
- The person you most trust to keep a secret.
- The person you feel shares the most with you.
- The person whose lifestyle is most like yours.
- The person with whom you've had the most fun.
- The person who hugs you the most.
- The person you can count on the most.
- The person who doesn't criticize you.
- The person you consider to be the most positive.
- The person who laughs with you the most.
- The person you think takes best care of himself/ herself.
- The person who listens to you the most.
- The person who talks the least about other people's problems.
- The person who always makes you feel good.
- The person who is the most active.
- The person who has the most hopes and dreams.

Next, place an "0" on the appropriate finger for the person who best matches each of the following statements. You will end up with 17 "0" marks scattered among the fingers.

- The person who has the worst health.
- The person who is the unhappiest.
- The person who smokes or drinks the most.
- The person who worries the most.
- The person who is sick most often.
- The person who complains the most.
- The person who hangs on you the most.
- The person who has had the most loss in his/her life.
- The person who gets angry most often.
- The person who tells you the most about his/her problems.
- The person who has let you down the most.
- The person who makes the worst choices in friends or mates.
- The person who borrows from you most often.
- The person who most frequently expects the worst.
- The person who is the most stubborn.
- The person who most often puts others down.
- The person who never seems to be happy with life.

HOW TO INTERPRET YOUR RESULTS

To identify your energy takers, add up the amount of "X"s and "O"s on each finger. The people represented by the fingers with the largest number of "X"s give you the most energy. The people represented by the fingers with the largest number of "O"s take your energy.

Look at the pattern of "X"s and "O"s.

- Are both marks fairly evenly spread among the four people?
- Do you have one finger with a lot of both "X"s and "O"s? A finger with few of either?
- Did you put any "X"s or "O"s on the finger representing yourself? (Aren't you your own best friend?)
- Most important, do you have an energy taker next to your middle finger? If so, why do you spend so much time with this person? How can you stop him/her from taking your energy? Why do you give your energy to this person? Does this say something about your overall relationship with him/her?

Exercise D

How Well Do You Nurture Yourself?

Take a piece of paper and cut a heart that is the size of your hand. As you read each question below, cut or tear off a piece of your heart that represents how much you feel you gave away during the past month.

- How often did you lose your temper?
- How often did you keep your mouth shut and not speak up for yourself?
- How much free time did you spend doing things for others?
- How much time did you spend solving another person's problems?
- How often did you skip a meal?
- How often did you do another person's job?
- How often did you stuff anger down inside yourself?
- How often did you go somewhere when you were sick and should have stayed home?
- How much junk food did you eat?
- How often did you tell yourself "no" when you could have said "yes"?

How much of your paper heart do you have left? Now, as you read each statement below, put back one or more pieces of the heart—enough to represent how much you gave to yourself this past month.

- Every time you said "No" to a person who asked for a favor.
- Every time you gave yourself some nurturing (hot-tub, music, flowers, book, exercise, etc.).
- Every time you spoke up for yourself.
- Every time you were able to delegate work rather than doing it yourself.
- Every time you played with friends.
- Every time you chose to eat healthy food.
- Every time you laughed.
- Every time you hugged someone.
- Every time you were alone and enjoyed yourself.

Do you have most of your heart put back together?

What did you discover by doing this exercise? How much of your heart did you give away? If you gave a lot, did you nurture yourself enough to stay balanced?

Think about what you can do to nurture yourself. When you give away too much of yourself, you can end up believing that people are just using you. This can lead to fear and anger. You may be afraid that there will be nothing left. Do you ask yourself, "But what about me?"

Of course, it is good to share and to help others, but not always at your own expense. If you have nothing left for yourself, then you have nothing more to give away. When you allow yourself to enjoy the abundance of life and share it with others, you create more abundance in your own life.

EXERCISE E

IDENTIFYING YOUR BELIEFS

Finish one or more of the following statements with
whatever first comes to mind. Don't think about it too
long. Now ask the question, "Why?" Answer that with
another statement, and ask the question, "Why?" again.
Do this until you can't give another answer. For an
example of how to do this, see page 120 in chapter 6.

It may be easier to do this exercise if you have
another person give you the opening statement and ask
you, "Why?" in response to each answer you come up
with. If you really push yourself, you may be surprised at
what thoughts come out!

Here are some sample opening statements:

- I wish I could have…
- My brother/sister never…
- One thing I believe is…
- I just wish I could…
- My job can…
- I get so tired of…
- Money is…
- I believe that my mother…
- I am so afraid of…
- It really makes me mad that…
- Just once I'd like to…
- If I had one dream it would…
- People who…
- It isn't fair that…
- My father was…
- I had a difficult…

EXERCISE F

CHECK YOUR BODY'S WISDOM

All objects in the physical world have a specific vibrational frequency—an energy "signature" of sorts. Our bodies recognize and respond to objects via this signature. Some health care practitioners have integrated this energy/response capability into their work. In fact, a field called Kinesiology has evolved recently which uses the body's energetic responses for diagnosis and healing.

If you would like to check this out, have a friend help you with the following experiment. It's a process called muscle testing. We'll assume your friend is a female for purposes of describing it.

First, gather several kinds of substances that your friend regularly ingests, such as pop, sugar, apples, cookies, cigarettes, water, beer, etc. Put them each into a separate bag. You can leave them in their original containers if you wish.

Ask her to raise one of her arms until it's at a 90-degree angle, i.e., shoulder height. Say to your friend, "I want you to keep your arm straight and strong each time I ask you a question. I'm going to try to push your arm down."

Next, test her arm response. Say to her, "Show me the answer 'Yes'." Her arm should stay up. Say, "Show me 'No'." Her arm will weaken and/or drop. (Even though the process is called muscle testing, this isn't about muscles and brute strength; it's chemical and electrical in nature. Just gently push her arm down hard enough to feel resistance.)

Now step behind your friend. Without her seeing what you have in the bag, hold it next to her body and ask, "Is this healthy for (your friend's name) body?" Then press the arm that is raised, and see if it stays strong ("Yes") or weakens ("No").

Continue to do this separately with each of the bags, keeping track of which ones generated a weak response and which ones had a strong response. When you have finished with all of the substances, let your friend know what her body "said."

Now, have her do the same process for you. The results? You will see the wisdom of our bodies.

Your friend's arm will probably become weak each time you ask her body about an unhealthy substance (e.g., pure sugar, alcohol, cigarettes). Unless she is allergic to a specific substance, her arm will probably remain strong when you ask her body about something that is considered healthy (e.g., water, fruit, complex carbohydrates).

One note of caution with this. Be careful how you ask the question; our bodies are very literal!! If you ask your friend's body if it **wants** something, her arm may remain strong even if that substance is obviously unhealthy. For example, if she is addicted to something like cigarettes or drugs, her body will believe that it needs that substance to survive.

Have fun experimenting!

EXERCISE G

THE TRAVELING WHITE LIGHT: A RELAXATION TECHNIQUE

I have taught the following technique to many people who wanted to learn how to relax. It really works! Read through the entire description, and then find a quiet space and follow the directions in your own way. You may decide you want to make a recording of it for yourself, or have a friend read it to you as you relax.

Lay down on your back with a small pillow under your knees and your arms down at your side. First, make your whole body tight and stiff and hard. Pretend that you are as stiff and tough as stone. Squeeze as many muscles at one time as you can, and hold that position for the count of 10. Now slowly release all your muscles and take in five or six slow, deep breaths. Allow your body to become soft and loose.

Now picture or feel a warm, glowing ball of white light floating just above your forehead. Imagine the ball melting into your forehead behind your eyes, relaxing every muscle, bone, and nerve. Relaxing even the tiny muscles behind and around your eyes.

Continue feeling or seeing the warm, white, glowing light melting into your face. Into your jaw. Relaxing your jaw. Relaxing every muscle, bone and nerve.

Feel or see the warm light traveling down into your neck. Relaxing every muscle, bone, and nerve in your neck. Relaxing your neck, and filling it with this wonderful warm, glowing light.

Now feel or see the warm, glowing light traveling down your spine. It is melting into and around every one of your vertebrae. Relaxing your spine. Relaxing every muscle, bone, and nerve all the way down to your tailbone. Then relaxing your tailbone.

Feel or see the warm, glowing, white light traveling from your neck into your shoulders. Relaxing every muscle, bone, and nerve in your shoulders. Relaxing and filling your shoulders with warm, soothing light.

Now feel or see the white light cascading down from your shoulders into your upper arms. Relaxing the muscles, bones and nerves. Relaxing your arms all the way to your elbows. Feel or see the warm, glowing light traveling down into your wrists. Relaxing every muscle, bone, and nerve in your wrists.

Feel or see the white light traveling into your hands. Relaxing and filling your hands with warm, glowing, white light. Feel or see the light flowing into your fingers. Relaxing every muscle, bone, and nerve in your fingers. Filling and soothing your fingers.

Now feel or see the white, glowing light traveling down from your neck into your chest. Relaxing every muscle, bone, and nerve. Relaxing your neck. Relaxing your lungs. Relaxing and filling your chest with warm, glowing, white light.

Feel or see the glowing light traveling into your intestines and all your organs. Relaxing all the muscles and nerves. Relaxing and filling your stomach and the rest of your abdomen with warm, glowing light.

Now feel or see the warm, glowing light traveling into your hips. Relaxing your hips. Relaxing every muscle, bone, and nerve. Filling your hips with warm, soothing light.

Now the warm, glowing light is traveling down into your upper thighs. Relaxing your thighs. Relaxing every muscle, bone, and nerve. Filling your thighs with warm, glowing light all the way down to your knees. Feel your knees relax as the warm glowing light encircles your kneecaps. Relaxing every muscle, bone, and nerve. Relaxing your knees.

The warm, glowing light is now traveling down into the calves of your legs. Feel the warm, glowing light filling your calves. Relaxing every muscle, bone, and nerve in your lower legs all the way to your ankles. Relaxing your ankles.

And now the warm, glowing light is flowing into your feet, into the arches. Relaxing all the muscles, bones, and nerves in your feet. Filling and soothing your feet all the way down to your toes. Relaxing and surrounding each of your toes. Relaxing and filling your feet.

Now the glowing, warm light is completely filling your body. Relaxing all the muscles, all the nerves, and all the bones in your body. Totally allowing every part of your body to relax. Relaxing from the top of your head all the way to the tips of your toes. Warm, glowing, white light is relaxing every part of your body. Relax. Relax.

Allow yourself time to remain in this relaxed state, breathing in and out very slowly. You may feel like you're floating. When you are ready to come back from this relaxation exercise, slowly open your eyes and give yourself some time to stretch and orient yourself to your surroundings.

EXERCISE H

THE COLORED BALLOONS: A TECHNIQUE FOR RELIEVING STRESS OR FALLING ASLEEP

This relaxation technique can be added to the Traveling White Light technique described in Exercise G, or it can be used by itself.

Imagine that you are holding onto the strings of several colored balloons. Each balloon represents and carries the feeling or energy you have toward something or someone you wish to let go of. Trust yourself to select the correct number and color of balloons; stay with your first thought.

Now focus on one balloon. Feel the emotions that come up with that balloon. Slowly let go of it. Watch it float up, way up into the sky away from you until you lose sight of it. As you release the balloon, imagine that it is carrying the emotion away with it. Feel yourself become lighter as you release it. Take in a slow, deep breath and exhale after you release the balloon.

Continue releasing all of your balloons in the same way. Focus on each balloon, letting go of them one at a time.

Don't be surprised if you fall asleep before you have released all of the balloons.

EXERCISE I

PUTTING THE PIECES TOGETHER

On the following pages are four stories—Ben, Jill, Dean, and Judy. Practice putting together the whole picture by reading each story and then answering the questions that follow. (My answers immediately follow the questions, but try to answer on your own before peeking!)

BEN

Ben is 17 years old. He loves to fix cars and even has a job working on them at a local gas station. Ben enjoys fast motorcycles, and his favorite drink is anything that has a kick to it. He is very uncomfortable at parties and hates big social events with a lot of small talk. He considers most of his classes in school to be boring except for physical education and psychology. Ben says that he's in love with a girl in his class who likes things to be her own way and has very little patience.

Ben and his girlfriend always get into fights because she doesn't like him spending so much time with his male friends. He doesn't understand why she gets so upset if he doesn't call or when he arrives at her house a little late sometimes.

Ben's mother is always trying to get Ben to do better in school. She spends a lot of time after dinner helping him with homework, but he rarely turns it in to his teachers. Ben's father is an attorney who appreciates Ben's ability to fix cars, but feels that his son needs to buckle down and focus on pursuing a "real" career. Ben is flunking most of his academic subjects. He says that he just doesn't feel motivated.

WHAT IS BEN'S PROFILE?

LEARNING STYLE: ○ Right Hemisphere
                 ○ Left Hemisphere
PROCESSING PATTERN: __ __ __
PRIMARY CONTROL TECHNIQUE: ○ Bully   ○ Accuser
                             ○ Shielder   ○ Whiner
BELIEF(S):

ANSWERS – BEN'S PICTURE

LEARNING STYLE: Right Hemisphere
PROCESSING PATTERN: KVA
PRIMARY CONTROL TECHNIQUE: Shielder
BELIEF(S): Ben believes that he will never meet anyone's
    expectations and that he will never be good enough,
    so he chooses not to try. He attracts people who
    enable him to continue to believe that he is not
    good enough.

JILL

Jill is a beautiful 29-year-old woman who never completed high school but always wanted to be a nurse. School was hard for Jill. She hates to read a lot of books and never liked to write papers. Jill loves to dance and enjoys exercising. She feels that it is very important to keep herself in good physical shape. If she gains any weight, she feels depressed and upset with herself.

Jill is in the process of divorcing a husband who is in a demanding profession in the public spotlight. Her marriage was fine until her husband started to take her for granted. He never listens to her and he always works late. He wants her home instead of working in some "cheap paying place."

Jill believes that she really worked at her marriage, keeping the house clean, cooking her husband's favorite meals, and making sure that she looked good for him. But no matter what she did, it never seemed to be enough. Her husband always found reasons to belittle her and abuse her verbally. "Do you always have to put mushrooms in my food? Why do I always have to remind you to do everything around here? Can't you figure things out for yourself?" Whenever Jill tried to confront him with her feelings, he would shut her out by ignoring her or saying, "I'm too busy to hear your problems now."

WHAT IS JILL'S PROFILE?
LEARNING STYLE: ○ Right Hemisphere
                 ○ Left Hemisphere
PROCESSING PATTERN: __ __ __
PRIMARY CONTROL TECHNIQUE: ○ Bully   ○ Accuser
                             ○ Shielder   ○ Whiner
BELIEF(S):

ANSWERS – JILL'S PICTURE
LEARNING STYLE: Right Hemisphere
PROCESSING PATTERN: KAV
PRIMARY CONTROL TECHNIQUE: Whiner
BELIEF(S): Jill's core belief is, "If I please you, you will
    love me." She believes that she has to be what
    another person wants her to be in order to be loved.
    This causes her to draw controlling men into her life
    who feed her need to please them.

DEAN

Dean is in high school. He says he hates school and that it is boring. He believes that his English teacher just makes his class read from books and write because she can't teach. He also believes that she hates him since she is always picking on him. He spends most of the time daydreaming in her class.

Dean's grades in all of his classes are "C"s and "D"s. He admits that he likes to put things off until the last minute and that he would rather be outside instead of reading a book. His teachers claim that Dean tries to get his classmates' attention by being the class clown. Dean says that he just enjoys making people laugh. He has been sent to the office several times for disrupting classes.

Dean says that his friends stab him in the back and that his brother always puts him down. Dean's father is only home on weekends, but he is patient. Dean likes to spend time hunting and just talking with him about almost anything. Dean's mother is always yelling at him and on his case. She thinks he's too sensitive about what other people think about him. Dean believes that his mother blames him for just about everything. She tells him that he is a lazy slob, like his father.

WHAT IS DEAN'S PROFILE?

LEARNING STYLE: ○ Right Hemisphere
○ Left Hemisphere

PROCESSING PATTERN: __ __ __

PRIMARY CONTROL TECHNIQUE: ○ Bully   ○ Accuser
○ Shielder   ○ Whiner

BELIEF(S):

ANSWERS – DEAN'S PICTURE

LEARNING STYLE: Right Hemisphere

PROCESSING PATTERN: KAV

PRIMARY CONTROL TECHNIQUE: Whiner

BELIEF(S): Dean believes that he is a victim. He believes that he is stupid, a failure, and that life is against him. He supports his beliefs by never putting forth his best effort and by playing avoidance games.

JUDY

Judy has a position overseeing a group of employees working on a production line. She takes her job very seriously and has great pride in her position. She worked hard to get where she is. She has a hard time with small talk, and she doesn't feel it's right to socialize with the employees that she works with.

To Judy, everything needs to be fixed—and she feels that she's the only one who can do it correctly. She is determined that everything in her department will run perfectly, and she leaves no room for excuses. Judy believes that if she doesn't keep tight control of the employees at all times, they will take advantage of her. Judy has had a lot of health problems and is a widow.

WHAT IS JUDY'S PROFILE?
LEARNING STYLE: ○ Right Hemisphere
                 ○ Left Hemisphere
PROCESSING PATTERN: __ __ __
PRIMARY CONTROL TECHNIQUE: ○ Bully   ○ Accuser
                            ○ Shielder   ○ Whiner
BELIEF(S):

ANSWERS – JUDY'S PICTURE
LEARNING STYLE: Left Hemisphere
PROCESSING PATTERN: VKA
PRIMARY CONTROL TECHNIQUE: Accuser/Shielder
BELIEF(S): Judy believes that she needs to control her
    world in order to be safe. She has the "Little Red
    Hen" attitude that she has to fix everything. When
    she is needed, she feels she is worthwhile. She does
    not trust others to keep her world safe, so she
    believes that only she can do things the right way.

EXERCISE J

YOUR WORK: WHY ARE YOU HERE?

1. Make a list of your thoughts and feelings about your work and where you are employed. Don't judge any of your thoughts; just write them down in short statements.
2. Now go over each of these items and organize them on a scale of 1-5, with 5 being the most negative and 1 being the least negative.
3. Now look them over, starting with the statements that have the highest numbers. Ask yourself the following question for each one: "If I am where I choose to be, why am I experiencing this?" Write down your response/reason next to each item.
4. Continue going through your statements until you have a response written next to each one.
5. Now, take each statement and response, and apply the technique you learned on page 120 in the chapter on Beliefs. Ask yourself "Why?" until you see the core belief under each of your responses.

For example, Bob was a foreman for a large company. For one of his statements, he wrote, "I hate my job because I am doing something that I hate to do."

When he went through the process of asking himself why he was experiencing this, he came up with the following sequence of answers. The belief underlying his statement may surprise you.

Why am I experiencing this? Why do I stay?
Because I'm the only one who can do it, I guess.
Why?
Because I guess I do it the best.
Why?
Because I am the best.
Why?
Because I always do my best.
Why?
Because I'm usually the one they count on.
Why?
Because I'm dependable.

Why?

Because I like to be.

Why?

Because I guess I like to be looked up to.

Why?

Because I feel important.

Why?

Because I feel like I'm needed.

Why?

Because they all need my help.

Why?

Because I guess I like them to.

Why?

Because I feel good when they need my help.

Why?

Because I like to be the one with all the answers.

Why?

Because I like to be the smartest.

Why?

Because when I feel smart they look up to me.

Why?

Because I like the feeling.

Why?

Because I like control.

Why?

Because it makes me feel good.

Why?

Because things are best when I'm the one in control.

Why?

Because I feel like I'm my best when I'm in control.

Why?

Because I don't like to count on anyone else.

Why?

Because I can't depend on anyone except myself.

Why?

Because they always let me down.

Why?

Because nobody really cares.

Is Bob really doing something he hates to do, or is he doing exactly what he wants to do? He wants to be in control. When he is in control, he feeds his core belief: "I can't depend on anyone except myself." He may say that he hates his job because it is stressful, but his job is fulfilling his need to have control.

When you discover the core belief behind a statement such as, "I hate my job," you can change the belief and create room for new opportunities.

EXERCISE K

CREATING YOUR PLAN FOR SUCCESS

Use this outline to create your plan for success. Start with a goal that is simple and can be achieved relatively quickly.

Begin by writing down your thoughts for each item below, and watch how your plan comes together. Don't agonize and take hours to fill it out. You can always go back later and add to it or revise it. The important thing is for you to make the commitment and get started. Unlimited opportunities are waiting to come into your life!

My Goal:

By When:

What I Will Gain:

Resources Available:

My Supporters:

Potential Obstacles:

Remedies & Options:

Action Steps to Achieve My Goal:

       Today:

       This Week:

       This Month:

       This Year:

My Affirmation: *"I believe in myself and I am successful. I am creating..."*

RESOURCE L

RESOURCES FOR HEALTH, EDUCATION & SUCCESS

PATCH ADAMS
GESUNDHEIT INSTITUTE

A medical project designed to address all the problems of one delivery system by not charging fees, not carrying malpractice insurance, not accepting third-party insurance, and being the first hospital devoted to silliness and humor in patient care. In addition, all healing arts are fully integrated; care givers live with the patients; initial patient interviews are three to four hours long; and medicine is integrated with arts and crafts, the performing arts, nature, agriculture, recreation, and social service.

Patch Adams
Gesundheit Institute
6248 Washington Blvd.
Arlington, VA 22205
Phone: 703-525-8169

EDUCATIONAL KINESIOLOGY FOUNDATION

The foundation specializes in Brain Gym® classes, workshops, and research, enhancing individuals' ability to learn through movement. The programs offered are most effective when combined with sensory integration techniques.

Educational Kinesiology Foundation
1691 Spinnaker Drive
Suite 105 B
Ventura, CA 93001
Phone: 800-356-2109

DR. DAVID FREDERICK
WORLD INSITUTE OF COGNITIVE SCIENCES

Dr. Frederick offers workshops and classes to help people enhance their mental and physical well-being. He combines knowledge of ancient healing techniques with modern psychology through the use of sound, energy, and music for physical and emotional healing.

Dr. David Frederick
World Institute of Cognitive Sciences
719 Olde Hickory Road
Suite F
Lancaster, PA 17601
Phone: 717-560-5609
E-mail: docdave@ptd.net

MARILYN KING

Marilyn's experiences as an Olympic athlete led her to develop an educational and corporate model that shows "ordinary" people how to accomplish extraordinary things. A successful speaker and presenter in the business arena for more than 17 years, Marilyn dramatically dismantles self-limiting thinking and behaviors. Her program, OLYMPIAN THINKING™, engages participants in expansive thinking and directed action. She also helps her clients to design processes and tools that create an environment for sustained peak performance.

Marilyn King
484-149 Lake Park Ave.
Oakland, CA 94610
Phone: 510-568-7417
Fax: 510-568-2310
E-mail: olympianmk@aol.com

RUDY LAWSON — "MR. RUDY"
MULTISENSORY ARTS AND EDUTAINMENT (MAE)
MINORITY PROGRAM SERVICES (MPS)

"Mr. Rudy," EDUtainer, offers multisensory tapes, materials, workshops, and conferences focusing on self-esteem and conflict resolution. A very talented performer, with a mission to promote world peace, Mr. Rudy's songs capture the hearts of young and young-at-heart audiences around the world.

Rudy Lawson
Multi-Sensory Arts and EDU-tainment
PO Box 571
Battle Creek, MI 49016
Phone: 616-965-6453
Fax: 616-969-9407
E-mail: mrrudyEDUtainer@aol.com

Minority Program Services
Phone: 517-629-2113

NUTRACEUTICALS

The neutraceutical Ambrotose® has been very effective in helping clients diagnosed with ADD/ADHD. Ambrotose® promotes cell communication, which can enhance an individual's ability to focus mentally and recall information.

Phone: 877-974-SELF
E-mail: learning@azuray.com

STEVE PLOGG
"I'M OK—YOU'RE ADD DEFICIENT!"

As a self-confessed, former "problem" student with low self-esteem, Steve is able to shed a positive light on what it's like to be diagnosed and labeled with ADD/ADHD. Steve tours the country helping students and educators to better understand ADD/ADHD, with a special focus on his Results Project.

Steve Plogg
620 Renaissance Point, #206
Altamonte Springs, FL 32714
Phone: 407-522-3741
E-mail: addsteve@mindspring.com

DR. WILLIAM SHAW
BIOLOGICAL TREATMENTS FOR AUTISM AND PDD

This book has proven to be very helpful for children who have been labeled as having ADD/ADHD, Tourette Syndrome, and symptoms of OCD. This book supplies the necessary information so readers can contact individuals who are available to help with the various therapies, including the gluten-and casein-free diet and the anti-yeast diet.

Dr. William Shaw
Great Plains Laboratory
9335 West 75th Street
Overland Park, KS 66204
Phone: 888-347-2781

RESOURCE M

TAPES, MATERIALS & PROGRAMS
AZURAY LEARNING, INC.

■ *RAP PAK MATH TAPES*
Written & produced by Mary Blakely. Music by Brian Drews and Brown & Brown Recording & Music Productions.

Four math tapes: Multiplication Rap Ups, Addition Rap Ups, Subtraction Rap Ups, Division Rap. These cassette tapes help children and adults who are primarily right hemisphere-dominant, kinesthetic processors to learn math facts. Each tape has a catchy rap beat that encourages listeners to slap, clap, and shake their bodies while they learn math. Nationally acclaimed as one of the best math tapes for students with ADD/ADHD, these tapes are used in many schools and homes throughout the United States.

■ *STARBRIGHT TAPES*
Three cassette tapes, designed to empower children. These tapes include songs and poetry that speak to the many emotional stages of growth and self-esteem.

Twinklers—Songs for ages 3–10. Words by Mary Blakely. Music by Richard Saroni and Brown & Brown Recording & Music Production.

Shooting Stars—Poetry by Kim Petrucci for ages 6–12. Music by Brian Drews and Brown & Brown Recording & Music Production.

Comets—Songs for ages 8–14. Words by Mary Blakely and Bill McNulty. Music by Richard Saroni and Brown & Brown Recording & Music Production.

All Rap Pak and STARbright tapes cost $10 each, plus $3.30 for tax, shipping, and handling per tape. Bulk orders are available; call for details. To order tapes, visit our World Wide Web site at www.azuray.com or contact:

Azuray Leaming, Inc.
P.O. Box 1748
Portage, MI 49081
Toll-Free Phone: 1-877-974-SELF (7353)
e-mail: learning@azuray.com
website: azuray.com

RESOURCE N

RECOMMENDED BOOKS

Ayres, Jean. *Sensory Integration and the Child*. Los Angeles, CA: Western Psychological Services, 1994.

Covey, Stephen R. *The Seven Habits of Highly Effective People*. New York: Simon & Schuster, 1989.

Dyer, Wayne. *Pulling Your Own Strings*. New York: Avon, 1979.

Fleet, James K. *Hidden Power*. West Nyack, NY: Parker Publishing Company, 1987.

Fleet, James K. *The Power Within!* Englewood Cliffs, NJ: Prentice Hall, 1994.

Freed, Jeffrey, and Parsons, Laurie. *Right-Brained Children in a Left-Brained World*. New York: Fireside, 1998.

Hay, Louise. *You Can Heal Your Life*. Carlsbad, CA: Hay House, Inc., 1987.

Hendrix, Harville. *Getting The Love You Want: A Guide For Couples*. New York: Henry Holt and Company, Inc., 1988.

Jampolsky, Gerald G., M.D. *Love Is Letting Go of Fear*. Berkley, CA: Celestial Arts, 1995.

Kline, Peter. *The Everyday Genius: Restoring Your Children's Natural Joy of Learning—And Yours Too*. Arlington, VA: Great Ocean Publishers, 1988.

Kline, Peter, and Saunders, Bernard. *Ten Steps To A Learning Organization*. Arlington, VA: Great Ocean Publishers, 1993.

Markova, Dawna. *The Art of the Possible*. Berkley, CA: Conari Press, 1991.

Markova, Dawna. *How Your Child Is Smart*. Berkley, CA: Conari Press, 1992.

Morrissey, Mary. *Building Your Field of Dreams*. New York: Bantam Books, 1997.

Myss, Caroline. *Anatomy Of The Spirit*. New York: Harmony Books, 1996.

Myss, Caroline. *Why People Don't Heal and How They Can*. New York: Harmony Books, 1997.

Pert, Candance, B., Ph.D. *Molecules of Emotion*. New York: Scribner, 1997.

Redfield, James. *The Celestine Vision*. New York: Warner Books, Inc., 1997.

Robbins, Anthony. *Awaken The Giant Within*. New York: Summit Books, 1991.

Ross, Ruth. *Prospering Woman: A Complete Guide to Achieving the Full, Abundant Life*. San Rafael, CA: New World Library, 1995.

Siegel, Bernie S., M.D. *Love, Medicine & Miracles*. New York: Harper & Row, 1986.

Vail, Priscilla L. *Smart Kids With School Problems; Things to Know & Ways To Help*. New York: New American Library, 1987.

Vitale, Barbara Meister. *Free Flight*. Rolling Hills Estates, CA: Jalmar Press, 1986.

Vitale, Barbara Meister. *Unicorns Are Real*. Rolling Hills Estates, CA: Jalmar Press, 1982.

NOTES

■ ■ ■

Chapter 1

[1] Whisler, Jo Sue, and Marzano, Robert. *Dare To Imagine: An Olympian's Technology*. Aurora, CO: Mid-continent Regional Educational Laboratory, 1988, p. 14.

[2] Whisler, pp.14-15.

[3] Whisler, pp. 15-17.

Chapter 2

[4] Hannaford, Carla, Ph.D. *The Dominance Factor*. Arlington, VA: Great Ocean Publishers, 1997. Hannaford, Carla, Ph.D. *Smart Moves*. Arlington, VA: Great Ocean Publishers, 1995, p. 181.

Chapter 5

[5] Redfield, James. *The Celestine Vision*. New York: Warner Books, Inc., 1997, pp. 71-105.

Chapter 7

[6] Adams, Patch, and Mylander, Maureen. *Gesundheit!*. Rochester, VT: Healing Arts Press, 1993, pp. 1-2.

ABOUT THE AUTHOR

Mary Blakely is the CEO and president of Azuray Learning, Inc., a corporation that creates, produces, and markets multisensory learning tools and programs. Azuray is based in Kalamazoo, Michigan.

Mary is a learning specialist, educator, author, professional speaker, radio show host, and clinical master hypnotherapist. In addition, she creates and produces learning tapes that are sold throughout the nation.

Mary has devoted over 20 years to teaching and creating educational and personal development achievement programs for children and adults. Her expertise has taken her into numerous schools and businesses, where she offers training seminars, classes, lectures, and individual and group consultations. She specializes in multisensory learning and training techniques, conflict resolution, teamwork, the mind/body connection, and the enhancement of personal potential. Mary works with gifted individuals, as well as those who are physically, emotionally, mentally, and academically challenged.

Mary is also a single parent of three adult children who has "walked what she talks." Her passion is to share her knowledge and experience by bringing awareness to those who are seeking greater success.